VIRTUE HOARDERS
The Case against the Professional Managerial Class

美德占有者
对抗专业管理阶级的案例

[美] 凯瑟琳娜·刘 ◎ 著

张焱　郑恩　[日] 千叶万希子 ◎ 译

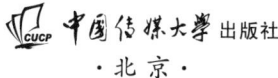中国传媒大学出版社
·北京·

本书受江西省教育科学"十四五"规划2021年度青年专项课题"'一带一路'视域下江西省留学生教育的跨文化传播实践研究"资助（课题编号：21QN001）和南昌大学"来华留学生教育的跨文化传播实践研究"项目（批准号：NCUCTWH202306）的支持。

先行者们的思考

这是一本在学术研究过程中思考写出的小册子,激烈的分析、质疑和推理是这本书的主体。

目　录

001　前言

015　"跨越"专业主义的边界

029　专业管理阶级的孩子

037　专业管理阶级的阅读

045　专业管理阶级的性观念

059　每个孩子都需要健全的国家体系
　　　丰富的童年应被视为一种社会福利

065　被捧上神坛的专业管理阶级

081　结语

087	Introduction
099	"Transgressing" the Boundaries of Professionalism
111	The PMC Has Children
119	The PMC Reads a Book
127	The PMC Has Sex
139	Every Child Needs the Good Enough State
	The richness of childhood needs to be embraced as a social good
145	The Apotheosis of the Professional Class
161	Conclusion
165	译者后记

前　言

正如我们大多数人都记得的那样，专业管理阶级（PMC）一直在进行一场阶级斗争，但这场斗争现在并不是针对资本家或资本主义的，而是针对工人阶级的。

专业管理阶级的成员们对他们在"进步时代"的快速发展记忆犹新。那时，他们支持工人阶级与强盗般的资本大亨进行史诗般的斗争，这些大亨的名字有：利兰·斯坦福夫人、安德鲁·卡内基、约翰·D.洛克菲勒和安德鲁·威廉·梅隆[1]等。但今天，人们去斯坦福大学，会发现以这些名字命名的私人基金会被视为参与慈善事业的典范，并且成为大学研究重要的资金来源，学者们争相通过这些基金会的赞助获得学术地位。虽然他们仍然相信自己是历史上的英雄，为保护无辜的受害者而战斗，对抗邪恶的加害者，但是工人阶级并不是一个他们认为值得拯救的阶层，因为按照专业管理阶级的标准，工人阶级的行为是失范的：他们要么在政治上脱离了控制，要么就是充满愤怒以至于失去了"公民"应有的体面。各个阶层中的自由派成员在谈论"人民"时喜欢使用"赋权"这个词，但这个词的使用从潜意识中是将那些被他们"赋权"的对象进行"物化"，暗示如果没有他们的帮助，人民就无法获得权利。

---

[1] 安德鲁·威廉·梅隆（1855—1937），美国金融家、慈善家，1921年到1932年连任哈定、柯立芝、胡佛三届政府的财政部部长。注：全书脚注均为译者注。

PMC作为当今统治阶级的代表，无耻地占有一切形式的世俗化美德：每当资本主义本身产生政治和经济危机时，PMC就会把事关改变政策与再分配的政治斗争改写为关于"回馈"的个人行为或自我改变的个体情感戏码。专业管理阶级在其独特的品位和文化倾向中找到了相对于普通工人阶级根深蒂固的优越感。如果说专业管理阶级的政治观点只不过是道德感的表达，那么专业管理阶级最善于利用的武器莫过于道德恐慌，以此来煽动其成员采取毫无意义的伪政治和监管形式。

备受诟病的希拉里·克林顿（Hillary Clinton）在2016年将唐纳德·特朗普（Donald Trump）的支持者斥为"可悲的人"，这种对普通民众的蔑视不可谓不坦诚。而这些"可悲的人"对PMC和自由派的对抗加剧了反权威主义，而其他类似于特朗普的反动政客，也正好利用了这一点在社会上煽动仇恨与对立情绪。

白领管理者一边削减蓝领劳动者的数量，一边鄙视工人在文学方面上的没品位、差劲的饮食方式、不稳定的家庭和糟糕的育儿习惯，在进行一系列贬低之后，他们最后还不忘"占有"美德，这无异于在工人阶级的伤口上撒盐。

PMC的历史并非一直如此。在PMC刚刚发展的阶段，其成员同情广大劳动人民的困境，开创了职业的研究标准（这些研究标准以美国医学会、大学教授协会和目前主导学术生活的所有专业组织为基础），以期通过保护专家群体的完整性来对抗资本家和市场的力量。从简·亚当斯[1]到约翰·杜威[2]，早期美国PMC成员建立了学术自由，他们认为研究在指导公共政策方面的

---

[1] 简·亚当斯（1860年9月6日—1935年5月21日），美国芝加哥赫尔宫协会的创始人。她因争取妇女、黑人移居的权利而获1931年诺贝尔和平奖，也是美国第一位获得诺贝尔和平奖的女性。

[2] 约翰·杜威（1859年10月20日—1952年6月1日），美国著名哲学家、教育家、心理学家，实用主义的集大成者，也是机能主义心理学和现代教育学的创始人之一。

作用与工业民主的发展同样至关重要。在这个过程中，第一批社会工作者、揭露黑幕的记者和激进的社会科学家正跟随美国工人和尤金·德布斯领导的社会党，为争取工人权利展开了为期一千年的斗争。

但这都已成过去，PMC的那些令人兴奋的英雄主义时光早已一去不复返。曾经的PMC拥有专业纪律和无私的光环，PMC在大萧条、二战以及战后大学扩张和美国社会经济秩序日益复杂时期，表现得非常出色。现如今，当潮流转向反对美国工人的时候，PMC开始与下层阶级打文化战，同时讨好它曾经鄙视的资本家。文化战争一直是经济战争的"代理人"，20世纪60年代，PMC以一种道德上似乎合理的方式将自己与经济上劣势的群体分开，将这个国家划分为所谓的开明国家和愚昧国家。

1968年之后，PMC逐渐将其所忠诚的对象从工人转向了资本。从那时起，PMC最成功、最引人注目的部分就是厚颜无耻地把自己的智慧用于为老板服务。如果说马克思认为阶级斗争是历史变革的引擎，无产阶级是历史变革的推动者，那么PMC的最新化身试图通过削弱工人阶级的权利、忽视工人阶级的利益来创造历史。1968年之后的PMC精英们已经在意识形态上确信自己的地位稳固，好似自己是地球上有史以来最先进的人。事实上，他们已经把"先锋精神"用反动的方式发挥出来了——利用曾经反主流文化的遗产及其对技术和精神创新的承诺，告诉其他人应该如何生活。在很大程度上，他们以自己的形象为标准，摧毁工人们的生活方式，建立起他们所心仪的日常生活中物质方面的基础设施。

随着PMC精英们财富的增长，作为一个阶级的成员，他们声称自己作为人类历史上文化和情感上最先进的一群人，需要坚持以不同寻常的、优越的、自我感觉良好的方式来做日常生活中的普通事情，例如读书、养育孩子、吃饭、保持健康。无论是赫尔曼·卡恩（Herman Kahn）、威廉·F.巴克利（William F. Buckley）、纽特·金里奇（Newt Gingrich），还是大卫·布鲁克斯（David Brooks）和塔克·卡尔森（Tucker Carlson）等，这些保守派成员对这个"新"阶级的批评，都纯粹是媒体导演的闹剧，但保守派成员谴责自由派对普通人的蔑视却是直击要害。右翼专家听到了普通人的愤怒，但他们把这种情绪武器化，用于反动的政治目的：没有人能像唐纳德·特朗普那样能有效地调动民众对PMC的不满，他利用几十年来保守派成功的宣传，将自由主义定位为人民和大众利益的敌人。特朗普从不装作有道德，他用与PMC相反的身份驱动（id-driven）的政治观点和缺乏自制力的表现，吸引那些感到被自由派的自大所蔑视的人。要打败伪装成民粹主义的反动政治，我们需要的是来自左翼的反PMC斗争，而不是像特朗普那样，用一种身份政治去抵抗另一种身份政治，因为身份政治本身已经成为承接PMC道德的一个载体。由此看来，民主党显然不是领导我们同资本主义及其破坏性极强的剥削和寻租制度做斗争的政治组织。

我对PMC的简要介绍是有争议的：对于这个术语新近的"客观"描述，你如果需要的话，可以看看加布里埃尔·温南特（Gabriel Winant）所作的《专业管理的鸿沟》，但也不要看得太多。

与温南特的文章不同，我的作品并不是一篇中立的专业学术文章，不是为了提炼术语及其定义，强调细微差别，然后对那些左派人士指手画脚。用温南特的话讲，那些左派的人是不文明的，甚至不能与之进行礼貌的讨论，这些人像扔导弹一样向敌人投掷各种绰号。温南特相信自由派的美德，而我不相信。2019年，在民主党初选开始投票前，伊丽莎白·沃伦（Elizabeth Warren）的民调是领先的，温南特为了给沃伦站台，发表了他抨击左派的文章。然而，在所有投票的州真正投票时，沃伦始终未能获得第二名，有时甚至连第三名或第四名都不是。温南特敦促桑德斯的支持者们"屈膝"接受沃伦所倡导的进步职业精神。但他没有预见到桑德斯反而会赢得一次又一次的初选，而选民们强烈反对沃伦的有限进步主义。

这种反对的原因是多方面的，其中主要的原因是，中间派和自由派无视民众对渐进式解决主义的不信任，忽视对激进经济重组的集体愿望。在美国，一代又一代据称中立的专家们掏空公共产品，诋毁公共领域，帮助从健康到教育等一切事物货币化，一代又一代负债累累的美国人幻想着精英主义可以增强社会流动性。实际的情况是，当金融资本和跨国企业鲸吞公共财富时，自由主义者只会作壁上观。温南特将PMC历史化，并要求我们不要放弃它的价值观。在评论PMC时，我对PMC的道德进行了批评性的描述，希望以此削弱PMC对我们思考政治的方式的影响。在本书的批评部分，我的结论是，希望社会主义的政治观点和社会主义政策回归，而这正是一度被PMC思想领袖所边缘化的内容，值得庆幸的是，伯尼·桑德斯（Bernie Sanders）在2016年和2020年的总统竞选中让其重见天日，这是具有历史性意义的。然而，现在我们已经看到了2020年民主党初选的结果，我更确信沃伦和PMC的其他成员将阻碍真正的政治变革。为了在新一届拜登政府中谋得一席之地，沃伦想要侧重表现的是她的职业优势，而淡化了她和桑德斯分享的政治意识形态和社会价值观。

约翰（John）和芭芭拉·埃伦赖希[1]（Barbara Ehrenreich）认为，PMC是由"不拥有生产资料的受薪脑力劳动者组成，他们在社会分工中的主要作用可以概括为对资本主义文化和资产阶级关系进行再生产"。

齐格弗里德·克拉考尔[2]（Siegfried Kracauer）和查尔斯·赖特·米尔斯[3]（Charles Wright Mills）将白领描述为不从事体力劳动的职员、销售人员和办公室工作人员。埃伦赖希则把PMC描述为由无种族歧视的、在大型组织中

---

[1] 芭芭拉·埃伦赖希，出生于1941年8月26日，是美国女权主义者，民主社会主义者和政治活动家。
[2] 齐格弗里德·克拉考尔（1889年2月8日—1966年11月26日），德国著名作家、社会学家、文化批评家，更是20世纪闻名于世的电影学者，也是具有世界影响力的思想家。
[3] 查尔斯·赖特·米尔斯，美国社会学家，文化批判主义的主要代表人物之一。

扮演重要管理角色的专业人士组成的阶级，如文化产业创意人士、记者、软件工程师、科学家、教授、医生、银行家，律师。在20世纪60年代，这个阶级中的年轻人把越战检察官罗伯特·麦克纳马拉（Robert McNamara）明确视为进步主义的敌人，是个冷血杀手，但从今天的PMC的定义来看，他是PMC中的一个非常高级别的成员。今天的PMC成员以机会平等、竞争、紧缩和效率的名义，居高临下地看着美国所有工人阶级和穷人糟糕的生活状况。自20世纪70年代以来，PMC精英们一直致力于放弃"大众政治"和重置社会分工，这无疑扩大了在资本主义晚期富人和穷人之间的鸿沟。

美国保守派比温南特这样的自由派更愿意谈论阶级对立。例如，在一篇名为《真正的阶级战争》的文章中，《美国事务》编辑朱利叶斯·克莱恩（Julius Krein）将美国当前的政治局势描述为0.01%的人和前10%的人之间的阶级战争，这个前10%的人即指PMC成员。对他来说，美国工人阶级被打压得根本没有所属的政治机构，因此，一个更好、更开明的PMC必须出现，以扭转在各个经济阶层加剧的不平等。克莱恩比温南特更激进，他敦促PMC精英们为自身利益而行动，反对精英们内部的不平等，且PMC的下层必须领导起这场反对异化和剥削的斗争，推翻其内部"可悲"的寡头统治者，美其名曰这是"为了帮助贫困的工人阶级"。在同一期的《美国事务》中，克莱恩还刊登了阿博·弗罗斯特（Amber Frost）的《管理阶层的无个性机会主义》，这篇文章与前面的观点相呼应，作者认为PMC是由不可靠的、变形的"后防兵"所组成。

2019年，迈克尔·林德（Michael Lind）出版了《新阶级战争：从专业精英手中拯救民主》。在这本书中，林德提出复兴美国无阶级社会的理想，他将白种美国人的民粹主义兴起归咎于专业精英，尽管我并不完全同意。林德还谴责了PMC妖魔化工人阶级对中间派渐进主义的拒绝。

林德是一个为工人阶级权利呐喊的反社会主义者。但奇怪的是，他一方面断言"占领华尔街"运动的失败，以及无政府主义与程序主义对阶级冲突的无视；另一方面他又幻想通过谈判解决阶级对立，保持阶级间的和平。他想要通过管理和行政的手段，而不是政治和客观的方法解决阶级冲突。林德与大多数中间派、保守派和自由派一样，害怕的是这样一种观点：即便是以政治治理形式真正实行了社会主义，也不意味着阶级斗争的结束，反而可能是它真正的开始。

作为一个阶层，PMC喜欢谈论偏见、种族主义、知名度；而对不平等、资本主义和剥削闭口不谈。宽容对他们来说是最高的世俗美德，但宽容几乎没有任何政治或经济意义。右翼深知自由主义的矫饰，它把民众对这一伪善阶级的怨恨化为自己的武器。右翼媒体福克斯新闻（Fox News）生为自由，但它对专业人士和专业主义的仇恨不是出于对人民的爱，而是出于对"自由市场"解决一切社会问题的特殊统治形式的忠诚。事实上，保守党需要一支强大的"在PMC中受到压迫而充满怨愤"的专业人士组成骨干队伍，来充当该党派的民怨政治打手。PMC继续迫使这些反动派背叛大众政策，比如放弃全民医保，转而选择经过智囊团研究、利润测算，由大型制药公司和说客背书的医疗保健形式，这种医疗保健形式允许以牺牲公共卫生和医疗保健工作者的利益为代价获利。自新冠病毒大流行以来，保险公司的利润翻了一番，因为它们最强的说客已将民主党玩弄于股掌之中。由此可见，PMC的遮羞布也沾染有金钱的颜色。

尽管PMC在本质上是非常世俗的，但它的修辞基调是伪宗教的。PMC在媒体上对自由、正义的垄断激怒了保守派基督徒，但它和大多数新教徒一样，从物质和世俗的成功中获得了救赎。在自由主义的圈子里，把谈论阶级差异或阶级意识形态放在首位，不仅是有争议的，而且是异端的。

如果你认为阶级是不能被种族、性别替代的概念，那么PMC成员会称你为"阶级还原论者"。他们用法律和各种各样花里胡哨的术语来掩盖对他们的唯物主义批评，他们不想让人们关注他们所代表的阶级身份和利益。年轻人如果想要从芭芭拉·埃伦赖希所称的"自由的职业"——学术界、文化和媒体行业——中获得职位，就必须适应由PMC势力圈子所把持的统一标准。

如果你想要对这个特权阶级进行批判，那你就会被假定为"赤化分子"，而且会被问到以下这些具诱导性的问题："你既然是社会主义者，为什么还要穿体面的衣服，你不应该穿些破衣烂衫吗？你为什么喜欢运动，那不应该是军工联合体的一部分吗？你为什么鼓励斗争，你难道想不负责任地煽动暴力吗？"

PMC精英们认为"左派"（社会主义者）就应该过苦行僧一样的生活，而且要为腐败、不公所致的社会冲突负责。PMC一方面宣扬对左派的偏见，另一方面又为资本主义的安定、奢侈与安逸辩护。加布里埃尔·温南特对左派挑衅的言辞，就是自由主义试图驯化那些反对PMC的社会主义对手的例子。左派必须接受的是，对我们社会主义者来说，没有阶级对立和阶级矛盾，阶级的概念就失去了意义。我本来并不想评论PMC，仅仅希望就我们的分歧进行一次文明的讨论，然而，以PMC为代表的自由主义者拒绝采纳和支持我们迫切需要的社会和政治变革，因此我写下这本书以批判PMC植根于历史、垄断道德的政治观点。

1977年，埃伦赖希富有创见地预言：在可预见的未来，PMC的价值观和意识形态将主导自由主义政治与新自由主义政治。随着权力的扩张，阶级及其定义性特征已经发生变化，资本主义变得更加富于掠夺性。事实上，PMC没有特定的政治意识形态边界，它像变色龙一样随时变成资本主义需要的"颜色"，最终构成了阶级结构动态变化的一部分。埃伦赖希（Ehrenreichs）的分析使我们能够孤立和识别一个资产阶级的霸权，PMC成员不顾一切地想要持续拥有自20世纪70年代以来积累的权力。PMC垄断专业知识领域的黑暗社会后果是，这个阶级霸占了公共道德解释权，以试图阻止任何有意义的经济再分配，同时也改变了我们目前的政治局势。

埃伦赖希借鉴了齐格弗里德·克拉考（Siegfried Kracauer）对柏林战时工薪阶层的研究，那个阶层是典型的被蒙蔽政治主体。这个阶层的人鄙视从事体力劳动的人，只梦想着暴富，为自己埋下了被解雇的伏笔。查尔斯·赖特·米尔斯谴责战后白领工人毫无希望地认同自身被商品化的身份，他指出，这些人作为某种特殊的工人，同样容易受到市场驯化及市场预设的、物化的人格和主体间性的影响。克里斯托弗·拉什[1]（Christopher Lasch）认为，白领阶层和管理阶层人员被他们自己的自恋所无望地集体催眠。对于埃伦赖希来说，过去的PMC体现了左派社会批评家所肯定的各种特质，但这个阶层的新精英们已经将他们对资本主义的认同武器化了。他们现在不但瞧不起大众的粗俗和愚蠢，而且对他们的自由先驱所捍卫的职业规范也完全漠不关心，甚至怀有敌意。他们实际上高度重视一种破坏传统和历史的企业家精神，这种精神能取悦公众，它讨厌等级制度和组织。

当你正在读这本书的时候，你可能和我一样，是PMC中一个矛盾的成员。我虽然是第二代PMC成员，但我并不喜欢我在这个阶级里看到的东西，因此，我决心要将PMC霸占的东西归还于社会，这些东西是美德、勇气、毅力、博学、专业知识、威望和快乐，以及文化和实际资本。要界定个体所属阶级变化的外形，就要进入艰难的政治自我批评过程，要剥离自己原有的价值观、情感和影响，进而残酷地重新概念化和历史化；放弃对知识分子或改良思想的拜物教式的崇拜，这一切都并不简单。这篇简短的前言在提供一些工具来向PMC防御最好的堡垒——政治组织、出版、媒体、私人基金会、智库和大学——发起攻击的同时，也帮助我们做出必要的自我批评。

---

1 克里斯托弗·拉什，美国著名历史学家与社会心理学家。其主要著作有《自恋主义文化》《最小的自我》等。

虽然表面上看起来是"右翼"阻碍着经济重组和大规模社会再分配，但实际上是持自由主义观点的PMC阻碍了政治革命，而政治革命是建立一个不同的社会和世界所必需的，在社会和世界中，普通人和工人阶级的尊严必须处于中心地位。伯尼·桑德斯本来打算在担任总统后实施再分配政策，PMC成员对此表示出敌意，因为他们不想让被压迫者们团结起来。相较于重新想象社会秩序的变革，PMC更倾向于让社会处于蒙昧主义（obscurantism）状态，巴尔干化[1]和在利益集团的管理之下。他们是无可救药的反动派，总是想扮演道德高尚的社会模范，而非被看作一个阶级。PMC的利益现在比以往任何时候都更多地依赖于它的企业金主，而大多数美国人的斗争以及苦难仅仅是PMC精英意识的点缀。PMC成员告诉自己，他们比其他人好，更有资格领导社会，以此来缓和他们因漠视集体苦难而产生的强烈内疚心理。

PMC中心主义是一种强大的意识，并且它在研究和创新方面的优先级越来越受到企业利益和利润的影响，而在人文社会科学领域，学者们由于受到私人基金会的奖励，普遍无视历史知识，更不用说历史唯物主义。遵守统治阶级的指令所获得的回报实在太大了，但是遵守这些指令所付出的智力和精神代价对所有社会成员来说也太高。在学术界，美国PMC在建立严格的同行评议共识和研究自主性方面取得了很大成就，但是PMC再也无力捍卫其所珍视的、用来对抗"极端主义"的知识中立原则。我们身处一个政治、环境、社会都有危机的时代，而涉及资源分配的阶级战争是我们这个时代的关键战役。

在《衰落的恐惧：中产阶级的内部生活》一书中，芭芭拉·埃伦赖希对1977年关于PMC的文章进行了后续研究，埃伦赖希认为，右翼分子对社会和公共服务界的攻击，当今反主流文化对普通人的蔑视，二者所致的经济

---

1 巴尔干化（Balkanization），指较大的主权国家或地区分裂为较小的、通常民族相似的国家或地区。

恐慌，导致了PMC阶级对工人阶级的敌意日益增长。到里根时代，嬉皮士已经演变成雅皮士[1]，或者说年轻的城市职业人士，他们可以夸耀信用卡带来的非凡享受和对即时满足的强烈依恋。随着自上而下的经济再分配结束，寻租的资本家形象在大众的印象中淡化，雅皮士占据了美国人民内心的中心舞台，成为社会的引领者，带领美国走向虚晃的盛世与自我放纵的未来。根据埃伦赖希的说法，雅皮士调和了20世纪60年代的享乐主义和80年代由债务推动的消费主义，手串变成了劳力士，但用来打破传统的内核都是一样的，即快乐会让你自由（pleasure will set you free）。这些年轻的城市专业人士嘲弄了经济上的无私性和精英对公共服务的理想，而这正是老一辈PMC成员的特质。无论是小说《美国精神病人》（*American Psycho*）中虚构的集流浪汉、妓女杀手、瘾君子身份于一身的华尔街交易员帕特里克·贝特曼（Patrick Bateman）[2]的作为，还是现实生活中唐纳德·特朗普的行为，都体现了纯粹的金钱权力的狂欢。在《美国精神病人》一书中，作者让雅皮士的虐待狂行为显得刺激、迷人。

到了20世纪80年代，精英阶层对美国普通中产阶级、中低阶层和工人阶级的幻想被雅皮士和嬉皮士共同建构，即普通人被困在呆板的稳定工作、延迟的满足感和社会一致性中。他们就像福楼拜笔下村里的白痴，但令嬉皮士和雅皮士恼火的是，这群白痴却拥有丰厚的养老金，享受着各种福利。如果嬉皮士痛恨工会为这群人与战后企业谈判所取得的稳定，那么雅皮士将会更进一步去付出实际行动来打破这种稳定，他们通过杠杆收购摧毁了提供终

---

[1] 雅皮士（yuppie）是美国人根据嬉皮士（hippies）仿造的一个新词，意思是"年轻的都市专业工作者"。雅皮士从事那些需要受过高等教育才能胜任的职业，如律师、医生、建筑师、计算机程序员、工商管理人员等。他们的年薪很高。雅皮士们事业上十分成功，踌躇满志，恃才傲物，过着奢侈豪华的生活。与嬉皮士们不同，雅皮士们没有颓废情绪，不关心政治与社会问题，只关心赚钱，追求舒适的生活。
[2] 帕特里克·贝特曼：一位虚构人物，是布莱特·伊斯顿·埃利斯的小说《美国精神病人》及其改编电影的主人公和叙述者。他是华尔街一位富有、物质主义的年轻投资银行家，但背地里隐秘地过着连环杀手的生活。

身保障的就业制度，从而导致蓝领和白领被裁。雅皮士不是美国的精神病患者，也不是典型的反社会者，他们无聊、焦虑、墨守成规，但他们确实代表了PMC精英的另一种面孔，他们为新主人服务，并享受着服务的回报。当杰克·韦尔奇（Jack Welch）在1981年接手通用电气时，他将"为股东利益负责的精神"人格化为一个超级雅皮士。韦尔奇依靠一批成本削减专业PMC人士，"通过裁员来提高股价"。在韦尔奇的监督下，超过7万名通用电气员工失去了工作，他的管理能力被商业媒体和世界各地的商学院广为赞誉。股票经纪人和高层管理人员在裁员方面所做的工作得到了回报。在雅皮士的帮助下，一个以公共性紧缩和私人奢侈生活为代表的资本主义新世界诞生了。在这个新世界中，全球化经济和现代化大都市被破败不堪的城郊所包围，离岸劳动力和闪电般"快钱"不停地到处流动。这些精英一边执行新自由主义的命令，一边吸毒，他们所谓的先锋主义只受到信用卡额度的限制。

里根（Reagan）越是撕毁社会安全网，在软弱的中产阶级看来，穷人数量就越是噩梦般地翻倍，因为中产阶级中的很多人无法与穷人足够快地拉开距离，以至于失去资产阶级体面而沦为穷人。PMC精英们通过统治阶级的眼睛反观他们自己，犹如自己看下面的阶级——随着社会向下流动成为一个可怕的现实，穷人被视为社会中可怕的"另一半"（非富即穷，中产阶级萎缩）。穷人在右翼的谈话中被种族化、妖魔化了。在里根时代，出现了一种关于贫困的新说法：穷人无法控制自己的冲动，他们不能够量入为出。这种叙事始于20世纪60年代，当时丹尼尔·莫伊尼汉（Daniel Moynihan）认为贫困是一个"文化"问题。客观地说，到了20世纪80年代，美国中产阶级成员极其担心会落入下层阶级，他们自己的财务状况正面临越来越大的风险。软弱的中产阶级在一个动荡的新时代，雅皮士们一方面被自己仍然是上层阶级的现状所催眠，另一方面又承受着即将落入下层阶级的恐惧。

这种经济冲突的文化解释框架掩盖了它的物质基础，过分强调文化研究而不是从政治经济学视角分析。弗雷德里克·詹姆逊[1]（Fredric Jameso）和其他马克思主义者在我们理解社会冲突现象时想出了一个"文化转向"（cultural turn）的概念，这个概念忽视了经济条件对领悟品位和影响力的重要性。到了20世纪90年代，那些在20世纪70年代获得博士学位的文化反叛者冲进了大学，并获得了终身教授职位。他们不太关注预算和行政管理，因为他们沉迷于自己对反叛文化的承诺，这些承诺包括：穿牛仔裤上课，抽大麻，和学生睡觉，听约翰·卡尔的音乐，同时也欣赏麦当娜的MTV视频。让·鲍德里亚告诉我们，一切都是拟像的，似乎风格（style）已经成为物质（substance）最重要的组成部分，而词语作为能指，却永远脱离了所指物。PMC成员对主流文化与普通人的对立情绪中混杂着对亚文化优越感的沾沾自喜。

1　弗雷德里克·詹姆逊,1934年4月出生于美国的克里夫兰,他的文学理论专著《马克思主义与形式》(1971)、《语言的牢笼》(1972)、《政治无意识》(1981)获得了极高声誉,被称为"马克思主义的三部曲"。

"跨越"专业主义的边界

1996年,杂志《社会文本》(*Social Text*)接受并发表了艾伦·索卡尔(Alan sokal)的《超越界线:走向量子引力的超形式解释学》(Transgressing the Boundaries: Toward a Transformative Hermeneutics of Quantum Gravity)一文。编辑们认为这篇文章,来自我们今天所说的"觉醒"的物理学家和数学家。索卡尔引用了德里达(Derrida)、德勒兹(Deleuze)和瓜塔里(Guattari)等理论家的理论,并做出了以下令人震惊的结论。

> 20世纪的科学在深层次上的观念转变已经破坏了笛卡尔—牛顿式的形而上学;科学史和科学哲学中的修正主义研究也进一步质疑了科学的可靠性;最近,女权主义和后结构主义的批判已经揭示了西方主流科学实践中的实质性内容,揭示出隐藏在"客观性"神秘面纱下的统治意识形态。因此,越来越明显的是,物理"现实"实际上是不亚于社会"现实"的社会和语言的建构。

索卡尔的文章以掩盖了自由多元主义的后结构理论和激进相对主义的名义,否定了现代科学的基础——我们生活在一个由物理定律统治的世界,一个可以被观察和描述的世界。《社会文本》的编辑们,斯坦利·阿罗诺维茨(Stanley Abramowitz)、布鲁斯·罗宾斯(Bruce Robbins)、安德鲁·罗斯(Andrew Ross)和评审该文章的同行们急于支持混淆物理学理论的反启蒙作品，已经准备相信数学和医学上的对抗疗法正等待着被"理论"本身超越与革新。索卡尔关于量子物理学的文章似乎引入了一个新的由不稳定的跨越界限的亚原子统治的母系多元宇宙。这个宇宙正在影响着现实，准备冲击我们的思想，改变我们的性别观念（尤其是社会和文化方面的性别差异）以及品味文化的方式。

戏剧性的是，不久后索卡尔就自曝其文章只是一个骗局，意在揭示顶级文化研究期刊缺乏智慧和科学的判断标准，对此，编辑们则以傲慢、愤怒和保守的态度回击。索卡尔声称，后结构主义理论是一个欺诈性理论，它并不是基于任何学术研究或证据产生的，而是基于野心勃勃的作者们嚷嚷着的关于科学和客观性等的无稽之谈产生的。然而，《社会文本》的编辑们称，当他们第一次收到索卡尔的投稿时，他们认为这是个天真但值得鼓励的科学家，他有些笨拙但热情满满地试图去掌控理论。编辑们出于鼓励接受并发表了该文章（据称是出于鼓励他），之后，当他们发现索卡尔的文章是一个骗局时，他们对他进行了妖魔化。他们指责索卡尔的行为是不道德且充满恶意的。但事实上，这篇错误文章得以发表，编辑们难辞其咎。至少在学术界，它的发表严重损害了人文学科的声誉。而如今，从事量子物理学和量子化学工作的物理学家、数学家们仍在研究索卡尔事件。

理论家和人文主义者们尝试着忘记它。无论如何，它没有对期刊的编辑们造成任何事业上的打击。事实上，阿罗诺维茨、罗宾斯和罗斯在学术界的声誉反而变得更加显赫，因为他们声称自己正在进行一场正义的斗争，打击身份政治和理论的反动敌人。这三位编辑的观点代表了在学术界占主导地位、被PMC认可的身份主义者的立场。应该强调的是，索卡尔事件发生在美国学术界文化战争的高峰期，理论和文化研究的创新者们将所有反对认识论创新的人视为反动派，他们认为这些反动派试图坚持陈腐的观念，如客观性，或者更糟糕的——普遍主义。

就像艾伦·格林斯潘[1]（Alan Greenspan）和他所尊崇的安·兰德（Ayn Rand）等高瞻远瞩的新自由主义经济学家们一样，后结构主义文化研究理论家们鄙视二战后带有强权色彩的自由主义共识。这种共识的基础是国家和企业对终身就业者、劳动者、完善的社会服务和再分配政策的支持。新左派和文化研究者就像新自由主义者一样憎恨自由主义共识。如果你对此抱有怀疑，那就去20世纪90年代的关于文化研究的电子书籍中寻找相关内容，你会发现这种共识同父权制、异性恋正统主义以及模棱两可的福柯式"统治"思想一样饱受批判。20世纪90年代，在这种备受鄙视的共识基础上建立起的经济体系和社会安全网已因多年的企业掠夺而摇摇欲坠。正如伊丽莎白·沃伦（Elizabeth Warren）和特蕾莎·沙利文（Teresa Sullivan）在2001年出版的《脆弱的中产阶级：负债中的美国人》（*The Fragile Middle Class: Americans in Debt*）一书中所展示的那样，缩水的工资和不断上涨的生活成本迫使美国中产阶级为维持曾经的生活水平而背负债务。沃伦和沙利文表示，中产阶级已无法靠工资维持生活。为了在工资不再增长的情况下维持原有的生活水平，他们逐渐成为信用卡和二次抵押贷款等金融工具的剥削对象。中产阶级借钱不是为了玩乐，而是为了支付医疗费用、大学学费，以及自己或家人失业后创业的费用。在她们二人的书出版后，这种趋势愈演愈烈。经济增长已使大多数美国人支付不起买房的费用，但在20世纪90年代和21世纪初期股市动荡不安的情况下，房价仍旧在上涨。银行发现，只要房价持续上涨，中产阶级和工人阶级的抵押贷款债务就会成为它们尚未开发的利润来源。面对工资减缩的困境，美国人用他们的房子进行二次抵押，来支付爆炸式增长的生活成本。在早期，银行急于债务再融资和向几乎失业的人

---

[1] 艾伦·格林斯潘（1926年3月6日——），美国犹太人，美国第十三任联邦储备委员会主席（1987—2006），任期跨越6届美国总统。许多人认为他是决定美国经济政策的权威人物。

提供信贷：房主和购房者只需要薄薄一张纸质文件就能获得巨额贷款。而这些贷款将会成为次级抵押贷款市场崩溃的主要因素。在未来几年内，借款利率持续走低的情况下，民众受到鼓舞而购买昂贵的新房，然后用新买的房屋再次抵押贷款。银行以这些几乎是欺诈性的贷款（被称为次级抵押贷款）为工具，将良性的债务和风险债务转化为所谓的债务抵押债券。

当压力极大的房主开始拖欠贷款时，纸牌屋倒塌了。贝尔·斯登（Bear Stearns）是一家深陷高风险债务危机的投资银行，它在2008年3月耗尽了资金。雷曼兄弟（Lehman Brothers）在那年秋天破产，股市和房地产市场接连崩溃。富人指责在疯狂市场[1]下穷人蜂拥而入的行为——但我们知道，道德丧失和债务"文化"并不是造成这场危机的真正原因。我听到美国的富人抱怨，这场危机是穷人购买平板电视造成的。就像他们在镀金时代[2]所做的那样，富人再一次找到了在穷人身上寻求优越感的方式，但这一次，他们用的是更为廉洁的方式处理财富。事实证明，美国的普通民众被以政治腐败、经济金融化、工资减少、畏惧失败和缺乏监管为特征的黏性网络所困。对于约翰·卡西迪（John Cassidy）和亚当·图兹（Adam Tooze）等记者和金融历史学家来说，这场金融危机和随之而来的救济与世界各国中间派政府的垮台直接相关。

2008年9月10日，财政部部长汉克·保尔森（Hank Paulson）和美联储主席本·伯南克（Ben Bernanke）前往国会，敦促立法者拯救崩溃的银行业。2009年，在奥巴马政府的领导下，蒂莫西·盖特纳（Timothy Geithner）提出了TARP，即问题资产救助计划，为银行提供了7亿美元的公共资金来平衡它们的收支。根据图兹的分析，美联储向非美国银行额外提供了5万亿

---

1 虽然股票价值被高估，但是股票价格还会快速上涨，这被称为疯狂市场。
2 镀金时代（Gilded Age）被用来形容从南北战争结束到20世纪初的那段美国历史，有许多人在这个时期成为巨富，也因为富有，而过着金子般闪耀的生活。

美元，以保证全球金融的流动性。与此同时，在2007年至2016年期间，780万美国人因丧失抵押品赎回权而失去房子。经济危机和随后的救济在各个方面加剧了社会不平等，但金融部门也没进行重大改革。救济性银行依旧取消工薪阶层家庭的住房赎回权，同时拒绝向信誉良好的贷款人提供新贷款。在这位受过常春藤盟校教育的非裔美国总统的领导下，非裔美国人家庭破产了。事实上，众所周知，在2008年金融危机中，非裔美国人和拉丁裔房主受到的打击最大：到2018年，一个非裔美国人家庭平均拥有5美元的资产，而一个白人家庭平均拥有100美元的资产。奥巴马的身份政治并没有为少数族裔和工人阶级带来经济上的帮助。

在2008年的金融危机之后，约翰和芭芭拉·埃伦赖希在"占领华尔街"运动引发的抗议热潮中重提了于1977年所作的评论文章，并宣告了"雅皮士梦想的死亡"。他们给雅皮士的讣告为时过早且他们过于乐观，但这篇文章写于PMC似乎可以改变自身，与工人阶级团结合作的时刻。与之前的克里斯托弗·拉什（Christopher Lasch）一样，埃伦赖希夫妇强调PMC成员很难自我复制，因为他们在提高了阶层准入门槛的同时，也改变了所有美国人的工作条件。PMC家庭和他们的孩子正在高等教育的高额费用面前和精英腐败统治的狭窄大门前挣扎。埃伦赖希夫妇将希望寄托在占领华尔街运动上，他们期望此次运动能使PMC成为真正的现行政治的反对者。当抗议者于2011年9月17日占领华尔街的祖科蒂公园时，这些年轻的、向下流动的、受过大学教育的占领者毫无疑问地引起了全国的关注。两个月后，他们被驱逐出境，但这场运动阐明了一个描述经济不平等的定式："我们属于那99%的穷人。"这造成了1%的富人与那99%的穷人，甚至与穷人里最富有的9%（PMC成员）的人之间的矛盾。2012年5月1日，在一场由许多华尔街占领者参加的大规模抗议活动中，纽约市立大学研究人员露丝·米尔克曼（Ruth Milkman）、斯蒂芬妮·卢斯（Stephanie Luce）和潘妮·露易斯

（Penny Lewis）进行了一项调查，结果显示，活动人士和占领华尔街运动的参与者大多是受过大学教育的白领，且大多数是男性，只有8%的受访者称自己是蓝领。米尔克曼、卢斯和露易斯在分析占领运动时强调了核心活动家的经历，他们对加拿大反消费主义杂志《广告克星》（Adbusters）的追捧，以及他们从阿拉伯之春抗议活动（the Arab Spring protests）中所获得的灵感。

米尔克曼、卢斯和路易斯引用了一位参与者的话："OWS（占领华尔街）是漂浮的能指，每个人在其中看到的东西都不一样。"漂浮的能指[1]是后结构主义理论最重要的原则之一。这一概念以费迪南·德·索绪尔的语言学理论为基础，由克劳德·列维-施特劳斯应用到整个文化领域。对于索绪尔来说，语言符号与经验世界中的实体无关。索绪尔的结构主义理论指出意义是从客观差别而非主观判断中产生的，这一观点在人类学和文学理论领域产生了极大影响。对于索绪尔来说，所指（即概念）和能指（即意义的语言单位）的组合共同构成了"符号"。后结构主义学者采用了这种语言学的原则，并将其转移到哲学和文学中。意义可以"漂浮"于所指的世界：能指变得空洞且游离，与所指或实体分离。当"差异"取代了矛盾（用黑格尔或马克思主义的术语），成为连接语义并决定语言灵活性的关键时，双关语便成为一种思维形式。1994年，艾伦·索卡尔（Alan Sokal）揭示了将后结构主义思想"应用"到物理学和科学尝试中描述物理现实的愚蠢性，试图批判后结构主义的政治和文化思想。但在2012年，理论学习者乐于用索绪尔的语言学发现研究新千禧年中最重要的民众抗议运动。索卡尔事件未能打击到任何后结构派的支持者，因为那群受过理论教育的年轻人走上纽约市的公共场所抗议金融体系，这种金融体系实际上是与虚无缥缈的概念、激进多元主义以

---

[1] 索绪尔认为符号具有任意性，即能指与所指之间没有内在自然的联系，基于他的思想，雅克·拉康认为能指无法表征所指，两者为松动的任意关系，因而称漂浮的能指，滑动的所指。

及金融价值解绑的混杂的经济体系。虚无缥缈的概念使股票经纪人、金融分析师和占领者以一种复杂的方式来谈论价值、缺点、谎言和欺诈。

在同一组采访中，参与人员阿伦·古普塔（Arun Gupta）谈到了埃内斯托·拉克劳（Ernesto Laclau）和尚塔尔·穆夫（Chantal Mouffe）的等价链概念，即对每个人的不满都应一视同仁。拉克劳和穆夫的这种饱受争议的民粹主义理论并没有吸引到公众的眼球，但它造成了一种分析"新"政治体制的错觉。受过高等教育的占领华尔街运动的参与者们，沉迷于用程序规则、管理、讨论的手段就所有集体决定达成共识。他们根据一种被称为堆栈[1]的方式管理日常会议或全体会议。这种严格遵从程序主义的管理策略压制了对优先事项或政治的有效讨论，最终只促成了堆栈模式本身的完整。保护这种模式变得比回应民众的政治需求重要，即使这些需求可能会引起生活正被金融资本直接破坏的数亿美国人的共鸣。PMC和新左派对于群众运动的看法主导了"占领"运动的政治理想，并限制了其激进行动的有效性。从人口统计学和政治的角度来看，占领华尔街运动完全是由PMC精英主导的："改变主题"这个口号从根本上有力地支持了此次运动的政治观点，但关于该运动的人口统计数据描绘了一幅清晰的参与者肖像：向下流动，男性，年轻人，白人，受过高等教育，背负学生贷款和信用卡债务。占领华尔街运动中加入工会的研究生占主导地位。

到了2016年，PMC精英们变得更加崇拜金钱，更加蔑视普通人。作为巴拉克·奥巴马（Barack Obama）的继承者，希拉里·克林顿（Hillary Clinton）是PMC价值观和民主党精英的化身。在希拉里·克林顿的领导下，民主党不再关注工人阶级的利益，但早在她丈夫执政时期，这些工人阶级的利益就已被忽视。尽管克林顿善于调和矛盾，处事圆滑通润：在精心建立一

---

[1] 堆栈是计算机术语，是按照先进后出的原则运行的工作模式。

个多元的、吸引资本支持的总统候选阵容的同时，他权力的行使也包括保护资本主义。华尔街和硅谷的选民们将得到安抚。除了来自佛蒙特州的参议员伯尼·桑德斯，没有任何左派成员敢在竞选中与希拉里对抗。希拉里是PMC精英们梦寐以求的候选人，这也昭示着该阶级已完全接管了曾经代表工人阶级利益的难以控制的民主党。希拉里是一个所谓的稳操胜券者，一个有史以来最合格的总统候选人，一个拥护华尔街和统治阶级的女人，一个想要激励女孩成为领导者的前卫的伪女权主义者。希拉里的失败不仅打击了中间派，简单来说，还表明人们对PMC精英们虚伪行径的愤然抵制。由于右翼民粹主义的兴起，政治评论家们被迫从阶级形成的角度来分析这场选举。地理和文化的差异使美国产生了阶级分裂，因而他们认为这场选举失败也应理解为地理和文化的差异导致的。

从20世纪90年代开始，跨界的反专业主义已经成为PMC精英先锋队的思想鸦片。安吉拉·内格尔（Angela Nagle）的著作《杀死所有无聊的普通人：从外国综合性讨论区、轻博客网站到特朗普和另类右翼[1]的线上文化战争》（*Kill All Normies: On Line Culture Wars from 4Chan and Tumblr to Trump and the Alt-Right*）激怒了这些文化研究的跨界崇拜者。像索卡尔一样，内格尔是老左派的支持者，但与索卡尔不同，她并不是STEM领域（Science, Technology, Engineering, Mathmatics）的终身教授。写出被索卡尔戏仿的一类文章的学者们拒绝承认内格尔的地位。自由派学者们无法忍受自己对亚文化内涵的热爱受到质疑或批评，尤其是来自同时期初级学者的质疑或批评。自内格尔的书出版以来，为了批判其作品，加布里埃拉·科尔曼（Gabriella Coleman）不断贬低爱尔兰学者并将他们列入黑名单。内格尔在准学术界担

---

[1] 另类右翼，即持有极端保守或反对变革观点的意识形态组织，主要特点是反对主流政治，通过网络媒体故意散布有争议的内容。

任兼职记者多年，但与科尔曼，一名以研究Anonymou组织（一个黑客组织）而获奖的民族志[1]学家相比，她几乎没有实质上的权力或地位。内格尔认为，科尔曼2014年出版的《黑客、恶作剧者、举报人、间谍》一书是反映学术界狂热支持跨界行为及其反规范性敌意的一个例子。内格尔称，科尔曼[2]不再与其民族志研究对象——互联网挑衅者，如黑客"weev"、安德鲁·奥伦海默（Andrew Aurenheimer）以及在2012年因攻击AT&T（美国电话电报公司）而被判刑的黑客保持距离。科尔曼喜欢跨界行为，正如被索卡尔戏仿的那样，她在自己的书中滔滔不绝地讲述她和那些小众的网络名人之间的关系。科尔曼并不在意"weev"是反犹太主义者、新纳粹分子和极右翼网站Daily Stormer的网站管理员。与科尔曼相反，内格尔认为左翼应该拥护阶级斗争的正规力量，而不是和奥伦海默一样，做出亚文化越界和剥削人民的行为。内格尔支持以工人阶级为基础的大规模联盟和运动，反对亚文化至上的政治。她认为这种形式的政治破坏了未来长期斗争所需的团结形态。然而，跨界崇拜者们将世界视作一连串跨越边界的机会的组合，他们为虚无缥缈的概念和德勒兹[3]的观点而狂欢。对他们而言，反对他们的戏仿、公民异议、理性争论、矛盾和论战都是无用的。

事实上，索卡尔和内格尔所批判的——学术界对跨越"规范"的盲目吹捧——已成为一种"进步"PMC精英获取媒体关注的策略。在以推进反对工人、反对学术自由的议程为目标的私人基金会的帮助下，今天的学术型创业者们正在利用社会事业推进自己的议程。学术研究，至少在人文和社会科学

---

1 民族志研究包括了对特定群体的社会和文化生活的所有研究，它着眼于提供一个整体的观点和视角，对特定社会文化环境中产生的信念、态度、价值观、角色和规范进行理解和解释。
2 科尔曼是加拿大麦吉尔大学（McGill University）的人类学家，科尔曼为了研究黑客，专门搬到黑客聚集的旧金山，与黑客们同住了三年时间，进而完成了一部作品。
3 德勒兹，后结构主义者。德勒兹对一切中心化和总体化企图都发起了暴风骤雨般的攻击，无论这种总体性是哲学式的，还是机构式的。

领域，正在被统治阶级的决策巧妙地影响——有时会直接受到拥有巨额财富的个人的影响，或受该人名下的私人基金会的影响，或受到在媒体中半学术性的受该人雇佣的自由主义者的影响。而不明确的是，这些专业人士和机会主义者是否意识到了自身在破坏学术自由和职业自主权中所扮演的角色。

例如，一个曾经默默无闻的私人基金会——普利策中心（Pulitzer Center），参与了1619项目[1]，这使其成为关于种族、奴隶制以及美国历史性教学框架的全国议论的热点。据称，普利策中心"通过直接支持所有媒体平台的高质量新闻报道以及独特的教育和公众宣传计划，提高了人们对被忽视的全球性问题的认识"。普利策中心的最大资金支持者是普利策艺术基金会（Emily Rauh Pulitzer）和艾米丽·劳·普利策基金会（the Emily Rauh Pulitzer Foundation）。而劳·普利策（Rauh Pulitzer）是新闻工作者约瑟夫·普利策（Joseph Pulitzer）的遗孀。

2019年，普利策中心与《纽约时报》杂志合作，启动了由记者尼科尔·汉娜-琼斯（Nikole Hannah-Jones）主导的1619项目。该项目的启动是为了纪念第一批奴隶抵达美洲殖民地四百周年——美国的真正生日。1619项目内容于2019年8月被《纽约时报》收录，在媒体界引发轰动：收录它的《星期日泰晤士报》副本很快售罄。该项目将美国革命改写为奴隶主反抗英国废奴主义者的革命，官方论述，美利坚合众国首先应该被理解为一个为捍卫奴隶制度而建立的国家。汉娜-琼斯否定了在1776年之前实施君主制的英国没有参与反大西洋奴隶贸易的历史证据，也不承认殖民者本身在这个问题上存在的历史分歧。为宣传自身对国家的看法，她领导一群作家、学者和记者驳斥了美国殖民历史学家所做的研究，并将他们视作无可救药的极端

---

[1] 1619项目是《纽约时报》在2019年推出的项目，旨在以奴隶制的后果以及黑人对美国的贡献作为民族叙事中心，重塑美国历史。

种族主义者。

正如《社会文本》的编辑们和他们的同行热衷于打破20年前科学和数学界的规范一样，1619项目的主导者拒绝接受历史研究所得出的结论。然而，就1619项目而言，《纽约时报》并不是一份小型学术期刊：人们对于冒犯该项目的强大资助者和捐助者心存恐惧，而这种恐惧给人们讨论调查结果蒙上了一层阴影。该项目的主导者们拒绝所有的批评：他们认为自己的发现并未依赖历史学界整理出的档案证据和界内的研究共识。尼科尔·汉娜-琼斯借助她的新影响力和庞大的受众群，批判关于美国殖民地的公认的学术研究成果，并认为其带有浓重白人男性偏见。在由世界上最大的媒体公司之一所提供的巨额资金面前，这些经受实证的毕生研究显得不堪一击。

显而易见，强大的金融和媒体利益集团就是1619项目的背后推手，它们为该项目提供支持，使其敢于尝试改变人们理解和研究美国历史的方式。该项目中最重要的一点是，它希望在摧毁美国工人阶级联合的可能性的同时，在有关美国历史的教学与写作中消除历史唯物主义。世界社会主义网站（WSWS.org）上的社会主义历史学家一直是该项目最直言不讳与聪慧的批评者之一，但他们的工作没有得到一个联系紧密且利益交缠的基金会和媒体精英网络的支持或资助。该项目想要为读者展示一个显而易见的道理：工人阶级的团结是不可能实现的。少数媒体，包括世界社会主义网站，公开了这样一个事实：在历史学家的压力下，《纽约时报》和汉娜-琼斯已经悄悄放弃最初的说法，即1619年是美国"真正的建国时刻"。《纽约时报》和汉娜-琼斯没有撤回或更正主张，而是在项目的网站上悄无声息地弱化了最初的观点，声称该项目旨在集中展现奴隶制以及美国黑人对塑造美国身份特征和国家叙事的贡献。在1619项目网站上，早期夸张的言论没有留下任何痕迹，但世界社会主义网站的研究人员保留了原网站中有关论文的副本。

很少有人会停下来问，为什么如此强大、富有的捐助者和组织会投入这样一个有关历史研究的项目——一个引起备受尊敬的历史学家们强烈批驳的项目。1619项目重点关注种族和美国奴隶制的历史特性，而忽略了使奴隶制与其他剥削形式相媲美的历史和经济条件——奴隶制度和农奴制是两个前现代的例子，而工业资本主义的工资奴役[1]则是另一个例子。通过这种方式，该项目进一步强化了我们这个时代中宝贵响亮的自由主义口号：工人阶级之间的跨种族团结根本不可能实现，更不要试图建立对资本主义的普遍批判。参与1619项目的主要思想家们坚持认为不是阶级而是种族造成了美国基本的社会和经济断层。他们认为种族主义是一个跨越时代的存在，它已被写进我们的民族性格中。

这种观点与二战后受私人基金会支持的意识形态所倡导的美国多元化模式十分契合。从多元主义的角度来看，非裔美国人是一个独特而强大的利益团体，因为他们拥有特殊历史，他们应该为自己辩护，他们在极为残酷的美国奴隶制度下遭受了极端的痛苦，他们应当索要赔偿——他们没有必要与其他工人一起加入工会，这些工人的经历永远无法与他们的经历相比。其他群体，即西班牙裔美国人、拉美裔美国人、亚裔美国人、美洲原住民等，都可以独立地为他们的特殊利益辩护。他们只需要提供一个具有竞争力的叙事版本，展现自身历史的独特性，并找到强大的捐助者来支持他们宣传自己的独立事业。

20世纪70年代初，当去工业化和紧缩政策作为美国阶级斗争的手段变得越来越完善时，乔纳森·科布（Jonathan Cobb）和理查德·塞内特（Richard Sennett）在写《阶级的隐伤》（*The Hidden Injuries of Class*）时采访了门卫里卡·卡尔蒂德斯（Ricca Kartides）（化名）。年轻的社会学家发现，卡尔蒂德

---

[1] "工资奴役"被用来描述一个完全依赖于工资来保障拥有食物、衣服和住所的基本必需品的人，这个人没有其他类型的金融资产能够使他在就业中断的情况下获得某种回报。

斯每天都在为自己的工作和低下的社会地位感到羞耻。然而，仅靠他个人的薪水，他就买到了自己的房子，他的孩子将不必住在他打扫的大楼里。但在今天，像卡尔蒂德斯一样，仅靠工资买房养家简直是难以想象的。如今，年收入24,000美元的普通门卫，也许在表面上或形式上与年收入1,400万美元的普通CEO是平等的，但这种平等似乎是资本主义和自由民主政治对工人阶级开的一个残酷的玩笑。

门卫的平均收入和CEO的平均收入之间存在根本的物质上的差异，而这种差异对于每个不是资本家的人来说都是无法忍受的，但PMC精英们已经深深地内化了精英统治的价值观，以至于他们无法明白这种收入差异的激进性本质，也无法理解这种差异与其他形式的差异存在根本上的不同。随着社会和经济分层的加剧，这样的差异催生了一系列政治危机，动摇了过去50年来推行新自由主义、紧缩政策的中间派政府。正是在如此不稳定的政体和持续的政治、经济危机下，复兴的左翼不得不进行政治反思并提出能够满足民众需要的文化纲领。如果左派拒绝对过去进行更正确、更有历史根据的反思，即拒绝把当代阶级和文化冲突置于争取平等、尊严和解放等普遍原则的历史斗争背景下分析反省，自由主义者就不会支持我们。自由主义者已经抛弃了历史，因为他们相信自己优于过去的精英和当代工人阶级。PMC成员认为自己是有道德的先锋主义者，凌驾在历史形式和条件之上，跨越了界限，发明了存在和观察的新方式。我们很难与他们争论，因为他们不接受将有益的辩论作为一种增进知识的方式。对他们来说，每一场辩论都要站在道德的制高点，摒弃理智或政治因素。索卡尔未能阻止美国化的不顾史实的后结构主义路线在人文学科研究中的扩散。内格尔重新定义了跨界的概念，却被逐出了学术界。我对自身批判当今学术界的主流力量不抱幻想，但在我的职业生涯中，我始终不会停止批判反历史、反物质主义、反专业工作的机会主义形式。

专业管理阶级的孩子

对于PMC中的父母来说，从怀孕的那一刻起，就面临着一个又一个的"选择"，孩子拥有的"潜力"必须被最大化挖掘。PMC中的妈妈们在听着莫扎特曲子进行胎教的同时，还不得不挺着大肚子做孕期瑜伽。对于今天的精英们来说，准备生养孩子，仅仅是一个令人饱受折磨并且花费巨大的长远事业的开始。

PMC成员对于生育这件事，既恐惧又兴奋，因为孩子必然会放大社会竞争产生的焦虑。在宝拉·法斯（Paula Fass）看来，恐惧是当代中产阶级养育子女的显著特征之一，因为中产阶级父母会"想象一个不成功的孩子将来可能会面临什么"。拥有工作的PMC中的父母尽管拥有双人份的工资，这使得他们能够保持中上阶层的消费水平，但是就算有全职雇工的帮助，他们还是会因如何教育婴幼儿和如何适当地鼓励孩子感到压力巨大。孩子是非常沉溺于本能的生命，既受父母供养，又耽于享乐。他们弱小无力而又对快乐有着极度的渴望，这对美国精英阶层的清教主义构成了生存威胁。因此，想方设法把孩子培养成为成功的成年人是PMC育儿精神的主要内容，这一点并不令人惊讶。对PMC成员来说，40%的美国儿童是婚外孕的产物或不属于中上层社会，这些儿童被视为不值得被公众关注的群体。不需要成为一个社会主义者，你就能观察到在儿童保育、儿童健康和儿童教育方面，阶级特权以最具戏剧性和最极端的方式再现。

在朱迪斯·华纳（Judith Warner）的畅销书《完美的疯狂：焦虑时代的母亲》中，她谴责了当代中上阶层母亲的令人痛苦的、竞争性的完美主义思想。自从2006年华纳出版了她的书以来，她所描述的时代焦虑仍在加剧。梅根·埃里克森（Megan Erickson）认为，这些焦虑和恐惧的产生并不是没有道理的："2008—2009年的金融危机在很大程度上加剧了上层精英对所有劳苦大众的阶级斗争，而且即便在全国收入最高的1%的人群里面，内部分层现象也越来越严重。"

在美国最富裕的社区，育儿时尚已经成为热门讨论对象。持完美主义思想的PMC中的父母是讨伐"阶级形成"的先锋：他们会理所当然地瞧不起保姆（无论是长期保姆还是临时保姆[1]）、老师、祖母和其他家庭的父母，居高临下地告诉他们打疫苗、看电视、挠痒、玩布娃娃、打电子游戏、吃"香烟糖果"的可怕影响。那些最富有的美国人的孩子在私立学校就读，自新冠肺炎疫情以来，这些孩子线上通过Zoom[2]软件学习或线下享受全职私人辅导员服务和较小班级规模授课，从而减少了感染风险，最大限度地保证了学习效率和质量。

1900年左右，新兴的PMC开始从公共政策角度关注儿童的福利问题。正如朱迪斯·塞兰德（Judith Sealander）所指出的，社会改革运动传播了一种强大愿景，即政府应该在纠正社会弊病方面扮演更重要的角色，特别是在儿童保育和产妇健康方面。但随着20世纪的结束，PMC精英们完全变成了新自由主义者，并加入了右翼势力，发出对"大政府[3]"及其因为经济下行发

---

1 长期保姆在几个月或几年内每天照顾孩子，更像是中国古代家庭里的奶妈或奶娘，有些长期保姆虽然每周只工作几天，但她们要随时随地为家庭服务。临时保姆通常只被雇佣几个小时。
2 Zoom是一款多人云视频会议软件，为用户提供兼具高清视频会议与移动网络会议功能的免费云视频通话服务。
3 大政府对人民的生活、经济等的控制严厉，因为其广泛的官僚机构和侵入性的法规和政策，其被认为是侵犯公民个人权利的政府。

放的所谓的微不足道的"施舍"的谴责。

比尔·克林顿（Bill Clinton）于1996年提出的"个人责任和工作机会协调法案"，即福利改革，掀起了一场针对该国最年轻、最贫穷和最弱势群体的无情而持久的战争。为了获得领取福利的资格，贫穷的母亲必须找到并且保有一份工作，哪怕她微薄的工资无法支付儿童保育费。经济萧条和"个人责任"已经成为削减福利的紧缩政策的招牌，用来折磨那些在富裕社会中最贫穷的人。在美国，总是有足够的钱给富人减税，而永远没有足够的钱投入有关儿童及其看护人的社会项目。在儿童福利问题上，PMC精英们认为，社会盈余，即整个经济活动产生的剩余价值，应该由少数富人的孩子享受，而大多数工人阶级和贫困儿童及其父母则被置于惩罚、监视和吝啬的奖励环境中，过着水深火热的生活。

本杰明·斯波克（Benjamin Spock）在他的畅销书《婴儿和儿童护理》中建议，有战后焦虑的父母要相信自己能够顺利养育孩子。该书于1945年首次出版，当时正值婴儿潮[1]时代，刚刚出生的婴儿正在蹒跚学步。

斯波克博士是二战后美国最有影响力的育儿专家之一。他普及了关于快乐和投射[2]的精神分析思想，他在新的PMC身份形成中发挥了至关重要的作用。斯波克反对关于婴儿教育的传统观念，并告诉年轻的富一代蓝领和白领父母要相信他们的孩子。虽然斯波克警告他们不要听当下流行的育儿建议，但是他自己的育儿建议蕴含在一本当下流行的书中，这本书被誉为美国20世纪继《圣经》之后的第二大畅销书。斯波克博士也是一位直言不讳的反越战、新左派活动家。保守派指责他煽动反文化运动，鼓励年轻人成为自我放

---

[1] 在二战之后的1946—1964年间，美国共有七千五百九十多万婴儿出生，约占美国总人口的三分之一。如今这群人已经成为美国社会的中坚力量。

[2] 投射一词在心理学上是指个人将自己的思想、态度、愿望、情绪、性格等个性特征，不自觉地反映于外界事物或者他人身上的一种心理作用，也就是个人的人格结构对感知、组织以及解释环境的方式产生影响的过程。

纵的叛逆者，理由是他们的父母在育儿时期就读了斯波克博士的著作，因此对他们疏于管教。然而，斯波克博士提出建议时带有一种自相矛盾的语气，而励志文学的读者对这种语气可谓耳熟能详。斯波克博士曾不停地提醒他的读者们，他们自身才是最了解情况的人。"你可以阅读书籍和文章，但你学习的主要方法应该是有目的地去观察。这意味着要花费时间照料你的宝宝和倾听他的需求，而不仅仅是给他喂奶、洗澡。一定要相信自己。因为你知道的比你想象中的要多。"

在20世纪70年代，当PMC中的年轻人涉足"东方"宗教时，与传统观念相比，他们更注重自我探索，追求情感和性实验，并且将为了生存而结婚、生活在传统的双亲家庭中的工人阶级视为不合群的独裁主义者。今天，经过几十年的紧缩政策，工人阶级的家庭和亲属关系网络正处于崩溃的边缘。杰斐逊·科维（Jefferson Cowie）和珍妮弗·希尔瓦（Jennifer Silva）已经提到，今天美国工人阶级的家庭生活比PMC中同龄人的更不稳定，离婚和单亲的情况也更多。即使要结婚，PMC成员也很少和其他阶层的人结婚。PMC家庭已经成为一个名副其实的坚固堡垒，阶级特权就是在这里被传承的，但育儿假期的压缩，不断增加的医疗保健费用，缩水的工资，以及爆炸性增长的高等教育费用，让PMC家庭陷入了困境，他们害怕无法把自己的后代培养成最"成功"的孩子。在新冠肺炎疫情流行的时期，这种担忧并没有消失，反而加剧了。

2014年，耶鲁大学法学院教师蔡美儿（Amy Chua）和她的丈夫杰德·鲁本菲尔德（Jed Rubenfeld）共同出版了《成功三大件：三种不可能的特征如何解释美国文化群体的兴衰》，证明了马克思主义是正确的。不过在这本书中，作者的"物质生活条件"完全主导了一切。

2011年的《虎妈战歌》（*Battle Hymn of the Tiger Mother*）取得了巨大成功，这本畅销的育儿回忆录记载了蔡美儿为丰富女儿们的童年所做的尝试，蔡美儿的文学经纪人蒂娜·贝内特（Tina Bennett）无疑希望后续的书能够像第一本书一样飞速上架。蔡美儿的这本畅销书是一本恼人但非常有趣的读物。当《华尔街日报》以"为什么中国母亲如此优秀"为题摘录《虎妈战歌》的部分内容时，意味着"虎妈"品牌获得了成功。尽管她一再郑重声明她的书的内容和书名都体现了自我贬低和自我反思，但读者还是把她的回忆录当成了育儿指南。

蔡美儿和鲁本菲尔德以完美的婚姻同步论证了成功的"文化群体"有三大特征：优越感、自卑感，以及更好的自控力。最后一种品质，碰巧在部分群体中是十分缺乏的，如非裔美国人、墨西哥裔美国人或穷人群体，这也解释了为什么那些无法抵抗诱惑的群体不能获得成功。蔡美儿和鲁本菲尔德发表了带有社会达尔文主义色彩的贫困文化理论[1]，这个理论被重新包装，每隔几年就会被拿出来说事，以证明在大部分美国人心中，不平等现象仍然存在。根据这两位耶鲁大学法学教授（其中一位已名誉不再）的说法，在美国谁是成功人士？当然是一小群富有的功利主义者。在蔡美儿和鲁本菲尔德看来，美国没有政治，没有阶级，没有社会，没有团结努力，没有社会责任，只有"文化团体"在争名夺利。他们认为，如果人们想要生活在一个更好的世界，就必须废除"团体"的概念。如果在美国人所说的公平竞争环境中，只存在成功和不成功的个人，美国就会是一个更好的国家。

尽管鲁本菲尔德在职业上取得了显著"成功"，但他也证明了自己严重缺乏自控力。2020年8月，鲁本菲尔德因行为不端，对女学生实行欺压和性骚扰，被耶鲁大学法学院私下停课。最近，耶鲁大学法学院的学生要求将他永久辞退。一群学生正在向耶鲁大学校长彼得·萨洛维（Peter Salovey）请

---

1 贫困文化理论，用存在于贫困者中的价值观和行为模式，来说明物质贫困及处境不利的学生智商分数不高甚至学习成绩低下的原因，它被视为对文化剥夺概念的发展。

愿，要求将鲁本菲尔德从教师队伍中永久除名。

随着贫富差距的扩大，以及每个族裔的社会流动性的下降，PMC的家已经成为一个实验室，里面有越来越豪华和昂贵的育儿设备和高要求的育儿技术。现在，父母会教授孩子贿赂和精心设计的作弊策略，以帮助他们的孩子不惜一切代价取得成功。"校园蓝调"案[1]揭示了富有的父母向大学顾问瑞克·辛格（Rick Singer）支付了数十万美元，以把他们的孩子包装成体育特长生，通过"侧门[2]"进入大学的事实。这是统治阶级决心保证他们的孩子"成功"的必然结果。

来自上层社会的阶级斗争给所有美国儿童和他们的父母带来了可怕的后果，但是它对最贫穷家庭造成的损害是最惊人的。最近，城市研究所发现，儿童是美国社会中最贫穷的群体，22%的美国儿童生活在贫困中，而38.8%的美国儿童在他们的生活中经历过某种形式的贫困。非裔美国儿童所处的形势更加严峻，38.8%的非裔美国儿童生活在贫困中，75.4%的非裔美国儿童曾经生活在贫困中。

当PMC手中的育儿书在宣传精英父母为保证孩子的"成功"而采取的非凡措施时，D.W.温尼科特（D.W. Winnicott）赞扬了平凡的知心妈妈与婴儿的相处方式，这种方式有利于大多数孩子的心理健康，使他们能够享受游戏、创造力和美好时光。温尼科特对看护者有一个广泛的、不分性别的认知。不过，为了简洁起见，我在讨论他的想法时使用他采用的术语——"足

---

1 美国的富人阶级通过私人升学顾问，采取贿赂、作弊等手段，使子女进入美国排名靠前的大学。美国联邦调查局针对此事件进行调查，这一事件被称为"校园蓝调"案。

2 瑞克·辛格认为进入名校有三扇门。前门是凭实力考试进入名校，但这需要天赋与努力。后门是给学校巨额捐款，但这个价格并非所有富豪都能承担得起的。侧门分为两条路，一是通过各种手段，把客户的孩子包装成为体育特长生，再贿赂大学体育教练，拿到大学的体育特长生预留名额。二是通过让心理医生开具《学习障碍人群证明报告》，让客户的孩子单独考试，并且多出一倍考试时间，瑞克·辛格甚至可以让客户的孩子在他控制的考试中心考试，在那里有专人替考。因此，侧门比前门更容易进入名校，比后门花费更少，受到美国富人阶级的追捧。

够好的母亲"。

在学习照顾婴儿的过程中,"足够好的母亲"即使爱她的孩子,也并不会及时全面地满足孩子的需求,一个足够好但并不完美的母亲开始逐渐适应满足她的婴儿日益增长的身体和情感需求,但也会因为偶尔没有立即回应婴儿的需求而忍受挫败感。这些必要的失败反映了母亲对其他任务的专注,也是婴儿建立对挫折足够的容忍度,以及实现对自我和他人初步认识的机会。

在1964年出版的《儿童、家庭和外部世界》的导言中,温尼科特写道:

> 我想请大家注意的是,有丈夫支持的平凡的好母亲仅仅是通过照料孩子,就在个人层面和社会层面做出了巨大贡献。正是因为这种贡献是巨大的,这种贡献反而没有被认可。如果这种贡献被大众所认可,那么每一个神志正常的人,每一个觉得自己是世界的一分子的人,每一个认为世界是有意义的人,每一个感到幸福的人,都会产生对女性无限的亏欠感。如果大众认可母亲这一角色,那么这种认可所带来的结果是减少我们自己的恐惧,而不是增加对母亲的感激和赞美。依赖性蕴含在每个人发展的初始阶段,如果我们的社会不尽快完全承认这一事实,那么就一定会有一种恐惧,压抑和损害我们的身心。

从这段话中可以明显看出,温尼科特认为,对婴儿的照顾是一种社会公益行为,所有父母都会在婴儿襁褓时期尽心尽力地照顾他们。父母是无私的,他们对自己的孩子充满爱,并且愿意为了孩子牺牲睡眠时间:他们的无私为孩子提供了不可剥夺的安全感和迎难而上的勇气,帮助孩子在未知的世界中面对成长的挑战。因为过于穷困,有些压力巨大的父母会计算养育孩子所花费的金钱,要求孩子偿还债务,大家都清楚地知道我们生活的世界之所以会存在这种可悲的现象，是因为有政府的财政紧缩政策和经济不景气的整体趋势。

虽然很难想象曾经有一个时代，丰富的童年体验被认为是一种社会财富，但仅仅在60年前，温尼科特就把他的精神分析理论建立在社会大众对被抚养者及其照顾者负有集体责任和共同责任的理念之上。对于今天普遍害怕跌倒和失败的我们来说，1964年温尼科特面对恐惧所表现出的乐观态度，既鼓舞人心又令人担忧。在战后的英国，温尼科特支持社会盈余的再分配，这种再分配将使绝大多数英国人体验到童年的丰富多彩。他公开承认，他童年的快乐时光提高了他的观察能力、共情能力和竞争能力。这些品质和能力是人类财富的一部分，地球上的每个婴儿都应该享有学习这种能力的机会。温尼科特一直认为，支持婴儿监护者是一种社会担当和集体责任。一个国家只要有普通水准的基础设施，就能够为育儿提供充分的支持，就能够为那些老人、孩童、残疾人士的看护者们提供优质的服务，就能够建立再分配的社会民主制度。如果足够优秀的母亲能够作为一种文化的、集体的以及社会共有的财富得到珍视，我们就可以建立一个不害怕依赖性，或妖魔化依赖性的社会。我们可以创造一个世界，在那里，有幸福的父母和稳定的童年，没有孩子会以牺牲童年的代价来换取成功。

专业管理阶级的阅读

2017年1月16日，为了让读者准备好应对特朗普就职典礼带来的冲击，《纽约时报》刊登了角谷美智子[1]（Michiko Kakutani）为巴拉克·奥巴马（Barack Obama）撰写的人物评论。作为"首席读者"，奥巴马是PMC精英的典范。他不享受继承的财富；他来自普罗大众却被精英阶层发现和提拔；他是自由主义者梦想成真的典范。如果我们相信他的成就，那么我们就会相信，社会流动性是种族主义和不平等的"解决方案"。

当奥巴马的接班人希拉里·克林顿（Hillary Clinton）在2016年大选中输给唐纳德·特朗普（Donald Trump）时，《纽约时报》的读者需要慰藉。《纽约时报》发声："自林肯以来，还没有哪位总统能像贝拉克·奥巴马那样，用阅读和写作塑造了他的生活、信念和世界观。"用奥巴马自己的话来说，阅读让他"放慢脚步"，站在"别人的立场"思考，这是奥巴马在套用《杀死一只知更鸟》（To Kill a Mockingbird）中的英雄阿提克斯·芬奇（Atticus Finch）的话。哈珀·李（Harper lee）的这部获奖小说讲述了大萧条时期发生在亚拉巴马州梅科姆的一场私刑。在小说中，阿提克斯给他的女儿琼·路易斯·斯库特（Joan Louise Scooter）和读者上了一堂有关文学和同情心的重要一课："你永远也不可能真正了解一个人，除非你穿着他的鞋子走

---

[1] 角谷美智子，日裔美国人，1998年获得普利策奖，是《纽约时报》的书评家、著名的文学评论家。

来走去，站在他的角度考虑问题。"就像大多数自由主义读者一样，这样的理解是通过阅读行为进行的。在奥巴马总统任期结束时，我们看到了大量关于阅读文学如何增强我们同理心的研究出现。在一个被种族主义和暴力撕裂的世界，阿提克斯和奥巴马向我们展示了个人同理心和个人自我修养将带来正义和理解。对于自由主义者来说，这样的叙述让人安心：阿提克斯不仅温文尔雅、反对种族主义，而且是社区中德行最好的一员，也是PMC的一员。作为一名乡村律师，阿提克斯也成了野蛮和种族主义世界中正义的化身。

2010年，在《杀死一只知更鸟》这本小说出版50周年之际，美国国家公共电台（NPR）用一篇空洞的文章赞扬了哈珀·李的小说：其中一名采访对象特意强调，奥普拉·温弗瑞（主持人）（Oprah Winfrey）曾把《杀死一只知更鸟》称为"我们的国家小说"。20世纪70年代，《杀死一只知更鸟》只是一部宣传冷战、满足人们好奇心的著作，不过成效不怎么样。但在奥巴马政府为九年级开设的"共同核心"课程中，《杀死一只知更鸟》再次在二战后经典美国文学中占据了重要地位。奥巴马政府想要恢复20世纪60年代早期的高度自由主义，但只是在形式上恢复。尽管奥巴马有机会在公共教育领域投资新的联邦基金，特别是在他的第一个任期内，但他的政府不愿像1959年那样投入资金，当时是因为苏联发射了人造卫星，迫使美国人在科学（STEM）研究和人文学科上投入与苏联同等的资金。据称，这套共同核心课程是一位受过"良好教育"的总统——奥巴马实施的一套更明智的联邦标准，以改革其前任乔治·W. 布什（George W. Bush）以"不让一个孩子掉班"（No Child Left Behind）的形式推行的简单化的、标准化的应试联邦教育政策。然而，奥巴马的教育改革并没有刺激政府对公立学校进行大规模再投资。

黛安·拉维奇[1]（Diane Ravich）和梅根·基尔帕特里克（Megan Kilpatrick）都支持教育改革是一场针对工会工人和下层白领人士的持续战争的委婉说法。在营利性公司和非营利性私人基金会的支持下，教育改革家们开始制定新的考核制度，通过绩效工资和紧缩预算来奖惩教师，这引起了公众对美国学校现状的恐慌。在过去的40年里，政客们在他们的反工人阶级言论中一直把"学校辜负了我们的孩子"作为高明的新自由主义叙事策略，以此削弱教师在课堂上的创造力、智力自主权，攻击工会化的公立学校教师。学生教育成果的改善本应该与教师薪酬、小班级规模和充足的资金直接相关，但在克林顿、布什、小布什和奥巴马政府时期，教育改革的目的是惩罚那些让学生表现不佳的教师。从芝加哥到西弗吉尼亚州，学校教师工会的罢工是工人们不再忍受紧缩政策的第一个迹象。这并非偶然，近年来，教师罢工，社区和学生有组织的宣传，给予了意识形态混乱时期的劳工抗议行动一些希望。

值得一提的是，在20世纪80年代，比尔·克林顿勇敢地"站起来"支持教师工会，这引起了全国轰动，这成为中间派政客讨好保守派的策略之一。在担任阿肯色州州长期间，克林顿听取了智库精英的意见，提出了在不增加学校预算的情况下提高教育水平的建议。为了提高阿肯色州在全美50个州中排名第48位的教育水平，克林顿要求把教师测试作为一项法律通过，并答应以小幅增税作为补偿。传统基金会发现，阿肯色州市民要求将每名学生的资助金维持在5,400美元的水平，这表明公众的挥霍无度需要加以遏制。比尔·克林顿同意了。对自由派和保守派来说，一直以来，煽动对公共教育状况的道德恐慌是一种政治权宜之计。比尔·克林顿的独特风格能够将1968年后制度化的身份政治与对紧缩和削减预算的狂热结合起来，这使得最富有

---

[1] 黛安·拉维奇（1938年7月1日出生）是教育史学家、教育政策分析师和纽约大学斯坦哈特文化、教育和人类发展学院的教授。她曾任美国教育部助理部长。

的民主党支持者和共和党支持者都很高兴。

2011年，《哈佛商业评论》呼吁进行联邦课程改革，以鼓励增加创造性、挑战性、趣味性和团结性。此后不久，奥巴马总统聘请了耶鲁大学文学专业的戴维·科尔曼（David Coleman），他是一名评估"专家"，对未得到充分服务的人群"感兴趣"，监督"共同核心"中语言艺术要求的复兴。像所有的教育改革者一样，奥巴马和科尔曼对"提高标准"很感兴趣。他们是怎么做的？他们启动了一个名为"力争上游"（Race to the Top，简称RTT）的项目，其中包括对学生以及相应的对学校和教师的奖励和惩罚预算。无论"共同核心"和RTT在提高教育水平方面的效果如何，奥巴马政府还是让19.3%的5岁以下美国儿童生活在极端贫困中。科尔曼离开了他的政府职位，成为精英教育的大师，也就是大学理事会的首席执行官。大学理事会是一个高利润的"非营利性组织"，负责监管SAT、GREs、MCSTs和所有的多项选择题考试，通过将考生分为普通学生和优秀学生来预测他们未来的学术成就。

像奥巴马任命的其他人一样，科尔曼给政府带来了辉煌的成就。在耶鲁的每一个文学和英语专业的学生（包括本书的作者以及过去和未来的国家安全局特工，比如超级间谍詹姆斯·赫苏斯·安格尔顿），也包括科尔曼本人，都被灌输了这样一种观念：精读是人类智力活动的最高形式。耶鲁大学文学系创造并推广了以冷战为基础的新批评主义，它迷恋于对复杂的文本进行精读，它基本的方法论依赖于对社会、历史还有政治背景的否定，认为只有在目光短浅的细读下，一个顽固的、蛤蚌般的文本才会展示绚丽的"珍珠"。耶鲁大学和新批评家们痛恨任何形式的庸俗和简单化。在科尔曼的领导下，"公共核心课程"是对照文本精读的要求所塑造的。"公共核心课程"设立了一项新的联邦语言考试，令人生畏的DBQ，即"基于文档的问题"（document-based questions），带有耶鲁创造的"精读"的所有特征。可是"基于文档的问题"（DBQ）中根本没有"问题"。在《杀死一只知更鸟》的案例中，学生们被要求为一篇精心准备的论文提供基于文本的论据（有的问题是让我儿子回答这部小说是如何阐述"表明立场"的重要性的）。

所以答案是，阿提克斯·芬奇是梅科姆镇唯一有能力对抗疯狂的种族主义者的人：他带来了一场文明暴力，旨在保护正义人群组成的团体。哈珀·李的小说充满了对以可怕的尤厄尔为代表的愤怒的、不服管教的、追求享乐的贫穷白人的仇恨。伯里斯·尤厄尔，这个被诅咒的家庭里最小的儿子，带着满身虱子来到学校。伯里斯的妹妹梅耶拉也有严重的个人卫生问题和不诚实问题，这个被诅咒的家庭中的父亲鲍勃·尤厄尔，无法控制他自己对性、复仇和暴力的冲动。尤厄尔一家也靠公共援助生活，这并不奇怪。鲍勃性侵了他的女儿，并诬陷给非裔美国人汤姆·罗宾逊。虽然是梅耶拉父亲对梅耶拉实施的性侵行为，但她在法庭上作伪证，指控她心仪的男人罗宾逊。阿提克斯在法庭上成功地为罗宾逊进行了辩护，但尽管有证明罗宾逊无罪的证据，罗宾逊还是被判有罪。在他被定罪后试图越狱时，一群暴徒使用私刑处死了他。在小说的结尾，鲍勃·尤厄尔仍然对律师为无辜的人辩护感到愤怒，所以他试图杀死阿提克斯的两个孩子。在他试图行凶时，他被镇上的闭门不出的布·拉德利杀害。

在小说的开头，坎宁安一家，穷而高贵的农民，令人讨厌的尤厄尔的陪衬，用山核桃向阿提克斯支付了律师费。斯库特问阿提克斯："我们家是不是很穷？"阿迪克斯告诉斯库特，自己家很穷，但不像坎宁安家那么穷。阿提克斯向斯库特解释说，"骄傲的"坎宁安家的农场已经被全部抵押了，他们不接受公共援助。坎宁安一家是善良的穷人。尤厄尔一家是邪恶的穷人：他们接受公众的帮助。超过一半的美国儿童在他们短暂的一生中经历过公共援助，让他们读一本关于一个邪恶的、愿意接受公共援助的穷人试图虐待和杀害一位高尚、善良的律师的家人的小说，似乎有点残忍。如果贫穷的九年级学生认真学习语言艺术课，他们一定会因为自己的家庭愿意接受哈珀·李的小说所拒绝的东西而感到羞辱。

很明显,《杀死一只知更鸟》传达的信息支持了比尔·克林顿1996年的福利改革。就像克林顿在担任阿肯色州州长时攻击教师群体一样,他在担任总统时攻击福利制度和福利接受者。在创造更具惩罚性的社会支持体系时,克林顿和哈珀·李一样,宣扬了福利会给穷人带来依赖心理和腐败的观点。和李一样,他提出"值得救助的穷人"和"不值得救助的穷人"的理念。当比尔·克林顿将福利计划改变为TANF(Temporary Assistance for Needy Families),即"贫困家庭临时援助计划"时,他的幕僚把贫困儿童变成了"好人",而把贫困儿童的父母变成了应该受到惩罚的"懒汉"。新自由主义政策表明,社会安全网不但不会扶起自甘堕落的人,而且会阻止人们上进的行为。由于李对这种观点的支持,她获得了普利策奖、国家自由勋章(乔治·布什总统授予)和国家艺术勋章(巴拉克·奥巴马总统授予)。

小说预言了1968年后PMC的胜利:善良的律师和他正义的女儿在道德上的正直使种族主义的解决方案对建制派具有吸引力——致力于培养个人的同情心、读书习惯以及正义感。《杀死一只知更鸟》是冷战时期非常有效的反共产主义宣传作品,该书作者基于一种自由主义的幻想,认为反种族主义就是善良的白人保护无助的黑人,对抗邪恶的(贫穷的)白人。该书创造了一种美国自由主义的形象,成为国内外赢得人心的有力工具。

2015年7月,哈珀柯林斯出版社出版了《设立守望者》(*Go Set a Watchman*),这是《杀死一只知更鸟》的续集。评论家对《设立守望者》感到失望,不仅是因为它的写作质量,还因为它揭露了阿提克斯是三K党[1]成员。在小说中,阿提克斯向一名参加过童子军的人坦白了自己的身份,后者

---

1 三K党(Ku Klux Klan,缩写为K.K.K.),是美国历史上和如今一个奉行白人至上以及歧视有色族裔主义运动的党派,也是美国种族主义的代表性组织。

现居纽约市，正在亚拉巴马州的家中度假。尽管《纽约时报》和角谷美智子都担心李的粉丝在发现阿提克斯·芬奇是一个种族主义者后会经历苦涩的失望，但第二部小说证明了李实际上是一个矛盾的宣传者，而历史记载和档案证据早就证实，三K党成员和实施私刑的暴徒都是受过教育、富有的白人，他们是所在社区的"正直公民"，他们中的许多人，像阿迪克斯一样，都是受过良好教育的专业人士。

如果说李是想要揭示《杀死一只知更鸟》所宣扬的种族主义和精英形象的虚假，那角谷美智子则忽略了作者纠正历史的意图。事实上，角谷美智子在2016年对奥巴马和有思想的人的描述受到了纯粹的意识形态影响。奥巴马流于表面的同理心有明显的局限性。他驱逐的非法移民比之前任何一位总统都多。2008年后的银行救助计划拯救了银行家，但将数百万拖欠高利贷的美国人赶出了他们的家园。奥巴马是为华尔街的利益而执政的，他受PMC精英的指导，而不是为工人阶级和那些银行欺诈和渎职行为的受害者服务。奥巴马是否可能更同情摩根大通[1]首席执行官杰米·戴蒙，而不是那些失去了他们住房和生计的普通非洲裔美国家庭？

在想象中拥有独一无二的能力，能够在所有的竞争环境中保持平衡，为数量惊人的各种性别、种族、性取向、性别认同等群体创造平等机会的美国，机构越来越倾向于把奖励分配给脑力工作者，而把繁重的工作分配给那些遭受苦难和被排斥的人。事实上，自20世纪70年代以来，PMC精英们已经拥有了令人艳羡的经济水平和心灵的安稳，这是未受过大学教育的工薪阶层可望而不可即的。此外，正如安·凯斯和安格斯·迪顿所指出的那样，没有高中学历的中年非西班牙裔工薪阶层白人的预期寿命缩短，幸福感急剧下降，甚至已经呈现出有大规模公共卫生流行病的趋势。不幸的是，"绝望的死

---

[1] 摩根大通是全球盈利最佳的银行之一，拥有超过2.5万亿美元的资产，管理的资金超过1.5万亿美元。

亡"已经成为我们大家都更加熟悉的一个词。这毫不奇怪，COVID-19（新冠肺炎病毒）在有色工人阶级社区的致命性要高得多：PMC中的工作人员可以在家工作，这让他们在新冠肺炎疫情肆虐时期享有额外的健康优势。

在18世纪初，当其他人的劳动使欧洲资产阶级精英有了闲暇时间去用一种被认为是不公平的方式来培养闲情逸致时，这些上流的闲暇男女开始想象社交的新形式。今天的资本家和PMC精英们也在修身养性，但他们对自己"特权"的焦虑，让他们拼命羞辱别人，不知疲倦地摆出文化政治先锋的姿态和做普通人无法做到的事情。PMC精英们一直在自我试验：从在新地方主义的支持下回归生酮饮食，到只喝充满污水的原水，以及断食疗法。他们的自我放纵行为是一种伪善的节俭行为。在礼仪和新的相互称呼方式方面，PMC精英们开创了一种自由宽容的语言，而工人阶级还没有掌握这种语言。PMC精英们有意无意地羞辱他们的对手，并认为他们极度缺乏智慧、同情心和美德。

当角谷美智子采访奥巴马时，他重释了阿提克斯·芬奇关于如何不成为一个种族主义者的观点，PMC精英们神化了一种阅读模式，这种模式被建立的目的是在封闭和敏感的世界里，让人与人之间建立一套脆弱但在社会上清晰的联系。奥巴马、角谷美智子和早期的哈珀·李在向我们灌输美国多元主义价值观方面发挥了重要作用。在这里，美国多元主义被视为一个自上而下的体系，它将专业化、自由主义的自我完善的假设纳入其中。其他人，其他的经历，只是为扩展我们的同理心和感知力服务。奥巴马和角谷美智子教我们如何处理我们的文化遗产：我们应该拒绝他们代表PMC进行的好为人师的说教。我们应该把阿提克斯·芬奇这个人物角色当作一个政治项目来思考；而这个项目所在的那部小说，则是一个被精心设计的、用来宣传反福利国家、反社会主义的作品。阅读很重要，但不是以奥巴马和角谷美智子所希望的方式。

专业管理阶级的性观念

在爱之夏（The Summer of Love）运动中，先锋派认为自己发明了一种具有革命性的体验性快感的方法，然而事实上并非如此。他们认为自己是人类历史上第一批性探索者，现实却也恰恰相反。性一直是一件复杂的事情，但是在18世纪的欧洲，以法国为典型，大多数放纵派男性对待性自由问题十分认真，或通过科学调查报告进入那个可视的世界，去发现"上帝之死"和非欧洲文化的价值；或通过不同程度的犯罪来藐视基督教道义和亵渎圣礼。可以说他们是这场性革命的一分子，对于这场性革命的政治后果，这群人也非常清楚。

在18世纪，法国浪荡文学里充满了不为人道的性癖、恋足癖的详细描述内容和对性交乐趣的深入探讨内容。这场性革命让我们认识到，我们应该把许多关于性的现代理念的产生归功于萨德侯爵[1]。作为一个贵族阶级的叛徒和绝望的性变态，他是法国革命的支持者，他命运悲惨，一生中大部分时间都在监狱里写色情文学。阿多诺[2]和霍克海默[3]指出，现代欧洲关于性行为的揭秘就是开始于萨德对人类性行为的推论和对性快感无休止的探索时期。萨德在他的色情小说《闺房哲学》[4]中写道："法国人要成为一名共和党人任重而

---

1 萨德是法国贵族和一系列色情和哲学书籍的作者，其以所描述的色情幻想内容和所导致的社会丑闻而出名。
2 阿多诺是德国哲学家、社会学家、音乐理论家，法兰克福学派第一代主要代表人物，社会批判理论的理论奠基者。
3 霍克海默是德国第一位社会哲学教授，法兰克福学派创始人。
4 《闺房哲学》出版于1795年法国大革命时期，内容包含了对同性恋和享乐主义的探讨。

道远。"萨德指出，1789年法国大革命或许已经推翻了教会和君主制，但是若想要解放广大人民，破除封建迷信和压迫，就应该对更深层次的上层建筑进行变革。也就是说，应该平等地向所有人传授如何从自己和他人身体中获得快感的性知识。然而性自由在旧制度下一直是贵族的专属权限，绝对性自由属于那些宣称自己是无神论者的人。萨德便迫切渴望实现全民性自由，他甚至警告，如果革命者们没有打破人民对封建性道德的推崇，没有强制要求人民拥有性自由，那么教会和君主的权力随时会卷土重来，丹东[1]、罗伯斯庇尔和广大人民推翻教会和君主制的革命成就将付诸东流。总而言之，如果这场性革命没有按照解放人民的逻辑进行，就会发生反革命政变。

在《闺房哲学》中，一个叫尤金妮娅的15岁少女在经验丰富的放荡者圣安吉夫人的引领下揭开了男欢女爱的神秘面纱，圣安吉夫人教会尤金妮娅如何将性快感最大化。在这本小说中，萨德指出通奸、鸡奸、卖淫、乱伦和强奸都应该合法化。结果证明，他的见解并非全无道理。在今天的美国，婚前性行为和婚外性行为已然不再是禁忌，除了有极端信仰的宗教派别外，父母不再会因为孩子们婚前发生性行为而流下恨铁不成钢的泪水。此外，同性恋几乎在世界上所有的工业民主国家被合法化，同性恋婚姻在其中的很多国家也被承认合法。在这些国家，卖淫者再被视为异己，哪怕仍然被人们所唾弃，国家合法化措施也为那些性工作者带来了莫大的福音，这也是建立性自由和性启蒙社会的最后一步。在一定程度上，我们不能否认萨德是一个有政治远见的人，但并不是所有萨德认为是被压迫的禁忌都会被今天这个开明的社会所打破。关于他的性启蒙的黑暗面在任何情况下都不会为社会所接受，比如为了享受性快感而虐待他人。

在二战结束时，西奥多·阿多诺（Theodor Adorno）和马克斯·霍克海

---

[1] 丹东是法国政治家，法国大革命领袖，雅各宾派主要领导人之一，国民议会中山岳派领袖之一。

默（M. Max Horkheimer）认为，萨德现象是一个被用于证明启蒙运动极端冷漠的哲学体系，具体表现在将工人和奴隶无节制地工具化，毫无人性地对他们进行剥削虐待。阿多诺和霍克海默认为，18世纪的感性主义恰好与萨德现象形成对比。但这两种价值体系对资本主义的扩张是不可或缺的：行善主义掩盖了这个世界的本质已经由征服生命向创造利润改变的事实。

20世纪60年代的性革命者借鉴了启蒙运动，然而并没有承认他们西方前辈的地位，他们更倾向于创新性地引用东方性艺术。这些新左派性革命者认为，他们已经形成了一种新的获得性快感的性爱关系，并且想将这种关系向世界普及。就像他们拒绝富裕社会提供的那些廉价劣质的产品和微不足道的满足感那样，他们也拒绝了过时的性交方式。这些反主流文化群体和新左派不断尝试所谓小说形式的享乐主义——一夫多妻制，也就是书中描绘的一个富有魅力的男性与臣服于他的温顺女人们的形式。

女权主义者对新左派男性那些来自原始部落的滑稽行为感到十分不满，她们意识到女性必须从男人那里收回属于她们的身体，而这样做就必须切断她们与性爱的关系。当波士顿妇女健康书籍团体出版了一本妇女健康指南《我们的身体，我们的自我》时，她们指出该机构一直十分了解女性身体的奥秘，同时认为网络上批判女性的言论将最终促进女性性意识的完全觉醒。如果说萨德小说中的女主人公认为女性通过性快感本身实现性意识的觉醒，那么PMC女权主义者则认为对性知识的普及才能真正实现性解放。受过大学教育的新左派女性认为自己是性和社会生活方面的先锋。《我们的身体，我们的自我》一书中罗列了女性可以去尝试的很多事——学习修车、远足、划皮划艇等，这些都是具有重大政治意义的个人休闲活动。书中也说到女性需要了解自己的身体，因为男性总是排斥让她们接触到这个危险又刺激的世界。 当作者采访PMC女性时，发现她们对于去看妇产科医生一事怨声载道，因为那些医生草草看了看窥镜后就迫不及待地跑去看网球比赛，丝毫没有对看病妇女的责任心。然而作者忽略了一个事实，世界上大多数妇女根本享受不到常规的医疗保健。为了进一步改善医疗保健是 PMC "特权"这一情况，《我们的身体，我们的自我》的作者鼓励底层社会女性去探索体力劳动的乐趣，殊不知世界上大多数女性做体力劳动不是出于自身选择，而是出于生活需要。纵观人类历史，人们对于妇女一边挑水种地、打理家务，一边喂养孩子早已见怪不怪。当妇女生活在用不起电用不起自来水的家庭中时，她们不得不做这些农活以谋求生存，这些是受过大学教育的城市女性无法想象的——除非她们在休学年去底层体验过。工业革命只是为工人阶级妇女创造了更多或流水化或精细化的工作，但所有这些生产工作都是单调乏味又令人疲惫不堪的。

为了打压解放女性的妇女运动，20 世纪七八十年代的保守派制造了一场关于打破婚姻和家庭关系束缚的道德恐慌。但随着时间的推移，反主流文化的 PMC 成员并没有成为性浪子，相反，大多数受过大学教育的美国人不但拒绝滥交，而且排斥那些激进的非传统的性爱关系，正因如此，他们的职业生涯变得更加成功。随着收入的增加，他们越来越想要过上稳定的生活。而对 PMC 社会、经济地位的保护使得本就贫穷的工人阶级不得不做出更大牺牲。今天，我们发现未受过大学教育的群体的离婚率和单亲家庭数量在不断上升。而在 PMC 家庭中，无论是异性恋还是同性恋，他们往往比工人阶级更接受一夫一妻制和传统家庭价值观。这确实是价值观上的反向讽刺，甚至颠覆了文化战争的逻辑。

对于 PMC 的女权运动来说，性革命在某种意义上是一场信息和教育革命。这是一场可以通过阅读解放思想的革命。这是一场 PMC 将性高潮和性快感视为 PMC 道德和教学改革对象的革命（大家还记得 G 点吗？），要想成为这场革命的一部分，你就必须承认，PMC 精英人士的经历和生活是进行有意义的政治和文化活动不可或缺的部分。在 PMC 女权主义构造的性行为世界中，最好的性行为可以在开放包容的社会中进行：它将发生在一张舒适干净的床上，没有经济或社会焦虑的干扰，仅仅是为了享受这个过程。在这种最理想的状态下，女性可以按自己的方式满足性需求，同时向她的性伴侣传达她的需求和欲望。自此，良好的性生活将加强双方的联系，成为彼此沟通的桥梁。当然，这都建立在双方自愿的基础上。

与受到性启蒙教育的PMC形成鲜明对比的是，在20世纪70年代的流行文化中，工人阶级被困在厌女癖、恐同症、偏见和暴力之中，同时社会也忽略了他们的感受和性需求。相对于同一时期在好莱坞工作的新左派创意人士和自由主义者，工人阶级一直生活在性黑暗时代。其中工人阶级男性是毋庸置疑的独裁者，而工人阶级女性在不知不觉中屈从于父系权力。然而，在19世纪初这一事实发生了转折，工人阶级不可否认地成为反对资本家及其代理人的政治斗争的先锋，而1968年后，PMC也承认工人阶级确实是所有革命的先锋，其中也包括性革命。

在奥巴马执政时期，州政府开始积极参与具有进步意义的性管理。从2008年开始，在这位博学总统的领导下，PMC集中精力将自由主义者的力量汇聚到一起，将有关性运动集中在阶级形成最重要的场所之一的大学校园，尤其是精英大学校园。对性暴力和对性过度痴迷是美国清教主义的重要组成部分，其中性启蒙中的道德优越感又是PMC反主流文化遗产的重要组成部分。在奥巴马的领导下，具有优越感的PMC精英相比于关注经济犯罪，更加关注性犯罪——并不是在工作场所，而是在大学校园。那些自由主义者把注意力从经济再分配等国家政策转移到校园性暴力上。简而言之，奥巴马并没有在他上任后解散银行或改革金融业，而是希望利用他的选举胜利来消除大学校园里的性暴力。2011年，教育部民权办公室发送"亲爱的同事"一信给七千多个大学并警告它们，如果它们不采取行动来预防和补救校园性暴力和性侵犯，那么它们将失去获得联邦资金的资格。法律评论员承认，大学管理部门确实十分遵守这封信的条例。然而，许多大学Title IX办公室[1]并不遵循民主法治中"疑罪从无"原则，虽然建立了所谓的校园调查小组，但这些机构只不过是袋鼠法庭[2]。

与此同时，似乎是为了证实奥巴马政府必须出台新政策的迫切性，关于大学校园里性暴力和性虐待的耸人听闻的新闻开始出现在许多主流媒体上。在哈维·韦恩斯坦的帮助下，迪克迎合了他的自由主义观众对校园性暴力新闻的需求。2015年，在奥巴马时代性恐慌最严重的时候，韦恩斯坦公司帮助科比·迪克拍摄了《狩猎场》，该片讲述了美国高校的性侵事件及背后各种阴暗的利害关系，这部纪录片把大学校园描绘成年轻女性居住生活的危险之地。然而事实并非如此，2016年，安布尔·弗罗斯特引用了全国犯罪受害调查数据，该数据显示，未上大学的女性遭受性侵犯的可能性是上大学的女性的1.2倍。大学校园里的性暴力吸引了推崇自由主义的PMC精英进入文化战争的新战场，在这个新战场里，不平等、压迫、工作场所的性骚扰和歧视成为主要的低风险斗争点。打击校园性暴力让PMC更加坚信：只有像阿提克斯·芬奇律师这样的白领，才是与除经济压迫之外的低风险事件斗争的真正英雄。

《滚石》杂志[3]诞生于1967年旧金山摇滚乐盛行时代，曾报道了奥巴马时代最耸人听闻的校园性暴力事件。该杂志曾经是一个非常成功的推动摇滚乐传播的媒体渠道，它促进了中产阶级一代消费者购买力的不断提升。到2014年，它已经成为一家能在互联网上争夺眼球的主流杂志。然而，2008年的经济危机对该杂志的打击尤其严重。印刷杂志的广告收入在2007年达到顶峰，

---

1 建立该办公室就是为贯彻落实民权运动中通过的《1972年教育法修订案》第九条（Title IX of the Education Amendments of 1972），该部分明文禁止公立高校内性别歧视。
2 "袋鼠法庭"这个词是美国俚语，一个丰富多彩的词，用来形容在明显违反法律规定的情况下进行的不公平审判。
3 《滚石》杂志是美国一本半月刊杂志，杂志主要关注流行文化。

此后年复一年地稳步下降，数字销售和布什、奥巴马政府所谓的经济"复苏"计划都没有给它喘息的机会。所以当特约编辑萨布丽娜·厄德利揭露弗吉尼亚大学（UVA）的轮奸案后，简·温纳和《滚石》的编委会就迫不及待地发表萨布丽娜的文章《校园强奸》，这是完全可以理解的。

这个9,000字的故事从受害者"杰基"的角度出发，详细讲述了2012年发生在联谊会上的一起可怕的轮奸案。这篇报道在《滚石》杂志网站上获得了270万的点击量。当《华盛顿邮报》决定对杰基的故事展开专题调查时，很明显，厄德利并没有证据证实杰基给她的任何细节，这篇报道存在许多漏洞，比如《华盛顿邮报》的记者们发现，杰基声称自己被强奸的当晚，并没有举办派对的记录。2015年，该杂志发表了《校园强奸》这篇报道的摘要，并由哥伦比亚新闻学院的一个团队对它的新闻失误进行了详细调查。《滚石》和萨布丽娜·厄德利随后被联谊会和弗吉尼亚大学学生教务长妮可·埃拉莫以诽谤罪起诉。这种公然的职业失误行为所带来的更广泛的文化和政治后果是难以评估的，但右翼人士当然知道如何激起民众对"主流媒体"和专业记者的怨恨，这次失败的报道理所当然地成为他们大做文章的切入口。极右新闻网站"每日来电"对这个案件非常感兴趣，并对《滚石》和厄德利要面对的耻辱及法律问题幸灾乐祸。对于保守党和煽动愤怒情绪的极右翼来说，UVA的故事证实了他们的说法：自由派媒体中充满了捕风捉影、作壁上观的伪君子，他们都希望能从妖魔化年轻人的假新闻中获利。

在"爱之夏"运动已经过去50多年的今天，正在上大学的女性比她们之前的任何一代人都掌握了更多的信息和性知识，但她们似乎没有承担性的责任的能力，也比前几代女性更需要保护。没有负责执行《1972年教育法修正案》第九条（Title IX）的老师的帮助，她们不得不独自处理性自主和男性欲望。西北大学教授劳拉·吉普妮斯（Laura Kipnis）自诩为"左翼女权主义者"、"反叛者"、自由思想家，用她的话来说：我们正在经历一个新的性偏执时期。在她的著作《不受欢迎的进步：性偏执狂来到校园》中，《1972教育法修正案》第九条和对前西北大学同事彼得·勒德洛（Peter Ludlow）案件的调查是本书的核心。吉普妮斯在《高等教育纪事报》上发表了一系列关于西北大学和彼得·勒德洛案件的文章，对指控她违反了 Title IX 的卡夫卡式[1]调查进行了清晰、公正的描述。吉普妮斯的书前半部分是学生对勒德洛的指控内容，以及西北大学对勒德洛和吉普妮斯本人发起的 Title IX 调查内容。她在该部分的结尾指出，尽管勒德洛确有不当行为，但他的罪行不至于让他失去工作，吉普妮斯将勒德洛的不当行为描述为出于天真的孩子气，而不是原始的虐待和剥削。

在《不受欢迎的进步：性偏执狂来到校园》的后半部分，吉普妮斯总结了她成为 Title IX 调查对象后听到的许多关于 Title IX 被滥用的故事。由于吉普妮斯受到了这一指控，她成为校园女权主义者和活动家的攻击对象，但她不会甘于沉默，她是一个自由主义者，一个高级自由主义者，这是最优秀的自由主义者的一种。她相信大学里存在着激烈的讨论，她在文化制裁这种妖魔化行为背景下对滥用 Title IX 进行了陈述，这对任何敢于质疑大学性骚扰调查背后的私下协议的人来说，都是一个勇敢的行为。

对吉普妮斯来说，性偏执最糟糕的地方是它使我们"变笨"了。性恐慌提供了"一种智力僵化的公式"。她指责校园里的猎巫气氛破坏了大学的传统理想——大学应当是自由思想家的避难所，这些思想家现在正被"陈词滥调和恐怖的雪崩"所掩埋。吉普妮斯所珍视的理想大学是建立在平等主义社会的社会思想基础上的幻想出来的大学，在那里，学生和教授都是自由主义者，免于物质欲望的困扰。虽然这种理想在1945年至1972年间是可行的，

---

[1] 卡夫卡式指捷克作家弗兰兹·卡夫卡的写作特色，多体现为对社会的陌生感、孤独感、怪诞感与恐惧感和不确定感。

但不断加剧的社会不平等现象和不断增加的高等教育成本已经摧毁了这个世纪中叶的美国大学理念。在吉普妮斯想象的大学里，每个人都生活在富裕的社会里，这体现出她理想中的大学是要建立在知识自由基础之上。吉普妮斯成长于美国高等教育空前扩张时代的末期，她不知道职场现实或经济危机，因此她盲目自信又逞强。她与今天折磨学生的焦虑明显隔绝。她对当代大学生活中的那些智力低下的性偏执人群给予了过多包容。但是根据经验，职业和经济上的危机感是最大的思想障碍。

在《不受欢迎的进步：性偏执狂来到校园》的结尾，吉普妮斯在对大学生酗酒行为进行客观分析的同时，指出我们这个时代的道德恐慌与女性性欲的不完全解放有关。她认为，校园性行为的问题可以通过对男女进行更多的关于性矛盾、性自愿和性责任的教育来解决。如果对信息和"教育"的高估，实际上是新自由主义及其紧缩政策下日益严重的社会问题的一部分呢？如果高等教育机构的名额竞争越来越激烈，进入PMC的门槛越来越高，以及实际上助长性恐慌的原因，使我们更加愚蠢呢？社会将教育视为私人财富，并且将教育当作在越来越不稳定的世界中竞争的资产，这导致大多数年轻人觉得他们在大学期间似乎无法满足他们的好奇心或缺乏愉悦感。吉普妮斯所珍视的知识和性自由，是由一种贵族式的自由主义思想塑造的，这种思想产生于20世纪中期美国的经济再分配制度和平等原则中，而当代大学管理部门对这种思想既不理解也不支持。

奥巴马政府对Title IX的积极执行，与汉克·保尔森（Hank Paulson）和蒂莫西·盖特纳（Timothy Geithner）在2008年金融危机后，策划救助犯罪金融机构的方式截然不同。为什么奥巴马政府不给投资银行家和金融顾问写一封信，警告他们不要帮助客户逃避数十亿美元的税款呢？如果使用得当，这些税款可以再被投到公立大学和公共教育项目中去。如果给大型制药公司写一封信，警告它们整治农村地区倾销鸦片类药物的联邦法规即将出台，情况会怎样？如果给富国银行、高盛集团、美国国际集团、摩根大通、美国银行等机构写一封信，警告它们不要提供黑心保险和贷款去损害借款人和投资者的利益，情况会怎么样？如果给化石燃料公司写一封信，警告它们隐瞒碳排放和影响气候变化的后果，情况会怎样？在没有这些信件的情况下，我们不得不得出这样的结论：即使是在全球金融灾难之后，PMC精英们宁愿煽动道德恐慌，也不愿实施哪怕是最温和的再分配或进步的经济政策。

为了结束我们对校园内性恐慌的讨论，我们必须把话题转向埃玛·舒尔科维茨（Emma Sulkowicz）的故事。2015年，舒尔科维茨毕业于哥伦比亚大学，她的表演《床垫表演：背负那重量》帮助她获得了视觉艺术学士学位。舒尔科维茨的这个作品是为了演绎一个事件，即在2013年她对同校生保罗·侬格瑟尔（Paul Nungesser）的强奸指控并没有给他带来任何后果，他继续留在哥伦比亚大学就读。舒尔科维茨以这个表演表达她对此事的抗议，舒尔科维茨曾希望学校将他开除，但经过内部调查后，哥伦比亚大学发现侬格瑟尔对所谓的强奸没有责任。舒尔科维茨对这个结果感到非常愤怒，她在大学四年级的时候一直带着所谓的强奸事件发生的证据的床垫。舒尔科维茨的复仇主义权利意识，她对正当程序（自由主义法治的核心）的漠视，她对隐私（被指控的攻击者和她自己的隐私）的漠视，在她的演绎中得以呈现。

就像所有以耐力为基础的行为艺术一样，无谓的体力消耗是精英们从体力劳动的需要中获得绝对自由的一种表现。从这个角度来看，舒尔科维茨背着床垫的表演是对体力劳动的嘲弄。世界上大多数劳动者仍在进行体力劳动，在一天的工作中必须忍受身体的痛苦："选择"忍受是PMC主权的最终标志。不言自明，舒尔科维茨先客观化了她自己的创伤。这一表演让她在一定程度上脱离现实，但也给了她一个平台，在这个平台上，她可以获得曝光度、褒贬不一的评价以及知名度。她成为一位女性的代言人，公开了一段痛苦的经历，这使她不得不在大众面前剖析自己的内心。舒尔科维茨作为一名艺术家，一个PMC精英的孩子（她的父母是曼哈顿成功的商业心理学家），是在对后工业工作制度做出自己的回应，这是一种需要宣传自我品牌、不断赢得大众支持的行为。在追求正义的过程中，舒尔科维茨以将个人痛苦变成公众热点的能力而闻名。

互联网时代最臭名昭著的艺术家之一——瑞安·特雷卡丁（Ryan Trecartin）也通过近乎疯癫的表演来吸引流量。他表演的尽是些狂欢的、荒谬的、吸毒成瘾的事情，带着堕落和自毁的特征。特雷卡丁标榜自己是自学成才的、做作的、邋遢的工人阶级艺术家。舒尔科维茨的艺术里有一种对名声的渴望，而这种渴望正是特雷卡丁创作的全部动力，但舒尔科维茨在宣传给自己留下阴影的性经历时有着别样的目的：她创作的动力源于对依格瑟尔强奸了自己却能逃脱惩罚的失望。从哥伦比亚大学毕业后，舒尔科维茨被要求极其严苛的惠特尼项目组录取，并开始了长达一年的实习深造，她后续的作品继续以性方面的哗众取宠和传播艺术界的声望焦虑被人熟知，她被人熟知是从一段录像《这不是强奸》开始，录像记录了她被强奸的过程。她还被一位她称之为"惠特尼先生"的性虐专家绑在半空，当时她身着一件白色的比基尼，两边各印了"W"和"M"，我猜是"惠特尼博物馆"的意思。她对自己作品的空洞阐述只是在鹦鹉学舌，表达的还是老掉牙的有关女权的那一套，以及反击"身体羞辱"的必要性。

被行为艺术家玛丽娜·阿布拉莫维奇（Marina Abramovic）和《纽约时报》艺术版块评论家罗伯塔·史密斯（Roberta Smith）誉为天才的舒尔科维茨对自己在艺术界的成功表现出了矛盾的态度。在2017年，她扮作治疗师，在费城一家虚构的治疗中心（Healing Touch Integral Wellness Center）创作了一部表演作品。《巴斯托》(Bustle)¹杂志称赞她的新作品抵制了特朗普。

但两年后，也就是2019年，她出现在以"alt-light"为主题的 Cut Hanging 杂志中，这本杂志的主要读者就是她曾经最讨厌的男权主义者。舒尔科维茨回应称，已经对他们的观点持开放态度。她还声称自己已经厌倦了当代艺术，并且将放弃做一名艺术家。与此同时，保罗·依格瑟尔与哥伦比亚大学达成庭外和解，他还根据 Title IX，以性别歧视为由成功起诉了哥伦比亚大学。对于自由主义者来说，校园里的性暴力至关重要，因为校园是阶级再生产的重要场所，所有参与其中的主体都必须被合理化。而且PMC精英们喜欢在非涉及经济剥削问题的道德剧里扮演贤德的英雄。劳拉·吉普妮斯不必对眼前的事实感到惊讶——部分PMC中的年轻人不再将性视为愉悦身心和繁衍的重要活动。对于埃玛·舒尔科维茨来说，任何发生在她身上的事情都可以当作公共宣传和检察机关的素材加以利用。个人和政治之间缺乏边界，这是当代新自由主义对历史反主流文化进行新陈代谢产生的毒果。

如果哈维·韦恩斯坦²（Harvey Weinstein）的事件不在我对性恐慌的批评范围之内，那是因为茱蒂·坎特（Jodi Kantor）和梅根·图伊（Megan Twohey）的观点影响了我，他们关注的是职场上利用职权之便的性侵，这一点得到了这位前电影大亨手下无数受害者和员工的证实。如果我们能把对哈维·韦恩斯坦事件受害者的调查和关怀扩展到那些在远没有那么光鲜的工作场所受到剥削和虐待的工人群体，那就再好不过了。在坎特和图伊的报道中，受害者们因为韦恩斯坦手握他们事业的"生杀大权"而恐惧。很显然，性胁迫和经济窘迫是虐待事件产生的温床。如果我们大部分人不能摆脱因生

---

1 Bustle是一家在线美国女性杂志，创立于2013年8月。它主要刊登关于政治、美容、名人和时尚趋势的文章。
2 哈维·韦恩斯坦，米拉麦克斯的创始人，是当今世界电影界极有影响力的人物，有着"现代电影的挽救者"的美誉。2017年10月，哈佛大学撤回了曾于2014年授予哈维·韦恩斯坦的W.E.B.杜波斯奖章。2020年3月11日，韦恩斯坦被判入狱23年，纽约最高法院法官宣布，他将正式被注册为性犯罪者。

存需要而产生的经济恐惧，我们就不会有性自由或性快乐。如果韦恩斯坦没有对整个产业经济上和人脉上的掌控，那么他对女性的虐待就根本不可能实现。和萨德一样，吉普妮斯同样相信建立一个没有经济胁迫的性自由世界的可能——这个世界固然是令人向往的，但在当下，资本主义的塑造让两性缺乏真实交流，因而这也只能是难以实现的理想罢了。

每个孩子都需要健全的国家体系
丰富的童年应被视为一种社会福利

在经历了南北战争后,政府才为退伍军人和他们的亲属建立保障制度。政府对童年及其不可侵犯性的恐慌,以及对士兵、遗孀及其子女的集体责任感在第一次世界大战结束时增加。大规模移民、工业化和金融危机,也使得人们对社会弱势群体所遭受的苦难和剥削有了新的认识。简·亚当斯和尤金·V.德布斯等人领导了为劳动人民争取社会服务和公共福利的运动。

除了资本家外,工人在新世纪的曙光中还面临着一个新的对手阶级:老板、工程师、专家和广告商。芭芭拉和约翰·埃伦赖希在1976年的文章《专业管理阶级》中定义了这个介于无产阶级和资产阶级之间的中间阶级的突出品质,他们主张财富再分配,同时谴责工人阶级的消费习惯。在进步时代,他们在阶级斗争中的作用并不明显,但PMC开始通过开拓新形式的文化纪律和加强社会秩序来为资本服务。PMC坚信道德仲裁者的身份,以此他们建立了将塑造美国几代人的育儿文化规范。

本杰明·斯波克是这个新阶级中最有影响力的人物之一。斯波克普及了关于快乐和认同的精神分析思想,在PMC身份的形成中发挥了重要作用。他的畅销书《婴儿和儿童保育》(*Baby and Child Care*)于1945年出版,彼时正值婴儿潮的第一代开始蹒跚学步。斯波克建议大家即使初为父母也应该相信自己可以照顾好孩子。斯波克所提倡的遵循自然和直觉似乎是权威式育儿法的解药，但他的读者们，也是20世纪中期的消费者，想通过消费有关儿童发展的新思想寻求育儿保证。

富裕的新任父母兼消费者通过接受专家建议来打破严厉家教的传统，并以此将自己与老一辈人和工人阶级区分开来。尽管斯波克提醒父母们对老式和时髦的育儿建议都要谨慎看待，但他仍然将自己的想法包装在一本有吸引力的书中，这本书被誉为美国20世纪仅次于《圣经》的第二畅销书。即使在他的新左派激进主义达到顶峰的时候，或书中的反文化同情受到攻击时，他的批评者们也一直尊称他为医生。虽然斯波克博士不断提醒他的读者们，称他们有足够的知识，但他强调了PMC对专业知识的钟爱。"你可以阅读书籍和文章，但你学习的主要方式是进行有意义的观察。这意味着要花更多时间观察和倾听你的宝宝，而不仅仅是喂养和清洗他……然后要相信自己，因为你知道的比你想象中的要多。"

在19世纪70年代，PMC婴儿潮时出生的第一代逐渐崭露头角，开始涉足"东方"宗教的自我放纵和超越家庭关系的自我表达，他们将他们的蓝领兄弟视为落后的传统主义者。但是在今天，情况似乎发生了逆转。杰斐逊·科维和珍妮佛·希尔瓦等历史学家和社会学家已经表明，与PMC中的同龄人相比，今天的美国工人阶级的家庭生活更不稳定，离婚和单亲家庭的情况也更多。经过40年的资本主义攻击，工人阶级的家庭关系和亲属纽带正处于崩溃边缘。面对裁员和驱逐，工人们发现，建立持久稳定的亲属关系几乎是不可能的。

与此同时，受过大学教育的美国人更有可能和本阶级的人步入婚姻殿堂。在过去的50年里，PMC家庭已经成为一座名副其实的堡垒，阶级特权就是在此被传递的。对于PMC中成员来说，从怀孕的那一刻起，就面临着一个又一个的"选择"，未来出生的孩子拥有的"潜力"必须被最大化挖掘，而40%的美国儿童是婚外孕的产物，这些儿童被视为不值得被公众关注的群体。可以毫不夸张地说，阶级特权的传承，也就是埃伦赖希所说的"秩序的维持"，正在童年本身的配置中发挥作用。

宝拉·法斯在她的畅销书《完美疯狂：焦虑时代的母性》中写了这样一句话：恐惧是当代中产阶级育儿的显著特征之一。中产阶级父母会"想象一个不成功的孩子将来可能会面临什么"。朱迪思·华纳谴责了让当代PMC母亲痛苦的竞争性完美主义。自2006年华纳出版她的书以来，为人父母的焦虑持续增加。雅各宾派编辑梅根·埃里克森认为，这些焦虑和恐慌的产生并非没有道理，"2008—2009年的金融危机加剧了上层对于下层开启的阶级战争，即使是在美国收入最高的1%的人中，也会加剧阶级分化"。在经济两极分化、公共机构和福利坍塌、人民福祉受损的社会背景下，像"婴儿教育"这样的育儿时尚已经成为热门。

> 对于有钱人家来说，父母的焦虑很早就开始了，但初创企业和风险投资家点燃了他们对育儿时尚和技术的信心。

追求完美主义的PMC家长们是阶级形成的先驱：他们会毫不迟疑地羞辱保姆、老师、长辈和其他家长，因为他们认为疫苗、电子产品、玩具等会对孩子带来不良影响。在家长们看来，他们的孩子只需获得社会优越感并模仿成功者的经历就够了。

对于有钱人家来说，父母的焦虑很早就开始了，但初创企业和风险投资家点燃了PMC父母对育儿时尚和技术的信心。以美国国家卫生研究院（NIH）资助的猫头鹰智能袜子的开发为例，这是婴儿袜，可以在宝宝睡觉时监测心跳和氧气水平。它会不断收集宝宝的数据，如果它的测量结果出现异常，就会向父母的智能手机发送警报。2012年，政府和投资者都声称要大力改善美国婴儿健康状况，猫头鹰智能袜子这一项目从美国国立卫生研究院获得了300万美元资金支持以及2,500万美元的私募股权和风险投资。奥巴马时代的联邦项目非常提倡创业精神，以至于美国国家卫生研究院愿意用纳税人的钱来支持奥威尔"互联托儿所"的理念。

不管有没有智能袜子，我们是否有必要如此担心婴儿的健康？快速浏览一下世界银行关于5岁以下儿童死亡率的数据就会发现，在过去50年里，全球婴儿死亡率急剧下降。由于成功研制出了脊髓灰质炎疫苗和天花疫苗，以及在其他领域也取得相关进展，婴儿死亡人数已从1960年的每1,000例活产婴儿中的93.4例下降到2016年的40.8例。美国婴儿死亡率下降得也同样明显，从1960年每1,000个活产婴儿中有30人死亡到今天的6.5人——这一切都与猫头鹰智能袜子毫不相关。

那么，除了吸引拨款和风险投资之外，猫头鹰智能袜子还能做什么呢？它切断了父母和婴儿之间的正常交流，维持人际关系最世俗和最需要的东西变成了焦虑和育儿信息。奇怪的是，"猫头鹰"无法直接满足婴儿所需要的照顾：人们必须通过激活传感器、应用程序和智能手机来获知婴儿的需求。随着贫富差距的扩大，以及每个种族的社会流动性的下降，PMC家庭已经成为一个日益奢华的实验室，以供研究高新的托儿设备和要求苛刻的育儿技术。

自上而下的阶级斗争对所有的美国儿童和他们的监护人都造成了严重后果，但它给贫困家庭带来的损失更是惊人。最近，城市研究所发现，儿童是美国社会中最贫穷的群体，22%的人生活在贫困中，38.8%的人在生活中经历过某种形式的贫困。非裔美国儿童的数据更为可怕：38.8%的黑人儿童正生活在贫困中，75.4%的黑人儿童曾经历过贫困。

健全的育儿机制背后是国家的强盛，该机制是一种由再分配支持的社会民主体系。

尽管PMC的育儿时尚大大宣扬了育儿技巧，温尼科特仍然赞扬了平凡的知心妈妈与婴儿的相处方式，它让大部分孩子保持心理健康，使他们在玩游戏和享受美好时光的同时还能提升创造力。温尼科特对育儿者有一个非常广泛的、不分性别的认知。不过，为了简洁起见，我在讨论他的想法时使用他的术语"足够好的母亲"。"足够好的母亲"即使爱她的孩子，也并不会及时全面地满足孩子的需求，她也在逐渐适应忍受无法满足婴儿日益增长的身体上和情感上的需求而带来的沮丧感。这些必要的失败反映了母亲对其他任务的专注，并为婴儿提供了各种锻炼机会，包括如何正确应对挫折，如何建立自我认知和对他人的认知。《持有与解释》一书中描述了温尼科特最著名的案例研究，分析了一个没有自发性和激情的男人。他的妈妈不认同母亲对婴儿的需求无法做到完美回应这一观点，而是试图在她的育儿经历中做到"完美"。

在他1964年出版的《孩子、家庭和外部世界》一书中，温尼科特这样写道：

> 我想请大家注意的是，有丈夫支持的平凡的好母亲仅仅是通过照料孩子，就在个人层面和社会层面做出了巨大贡献。正是因为这种贡献是巨大的，这种贡献反而没有被认可。如果这种贡献被大众所认可，那么每一个神志正常的人，每一个觉得自己是世界的一分子的人，每一个认为世界是有意义的人，每一个感到幸福的人，都会产生对女性无限的亏欠感。如果大众认可母亲这一角色，那么这种认可所带来的结果将减少我们自己的恐惧，而不是增加对母亲的感激和赞美。依赖性蕴含在每个人发展的初始阶段，如果我们的社会不尽快完全承认这一事实，那么就一定会有一种恐惧，压抑和损害我们的身心健康。

在战后的英国，温尼科特支持社会盈余的再分配，这种再分配将使绝大多数英国人体验到童年的丰富多彩。他公开承认，他童年的快乐时光提高了他的观察能力、共情能力和竞争能力。这些能力是人类财富的一部分，地球上的每个婴儿都应该享有学习这种能力的机会。

虽然很难想象曾经有一个时代，给予孩子们丰富的童年体验会被视为一种公益，但就在50年前，温尼科特才在社会大众对被抚养者及其照顾者的集体责任和相互责任的理念基础上，建立了精神分析理论。健全的养育子女的机制的背后是国家的强盛，是一种社会民主的再分配支持体系。

如果足够优秀的母亲能够作为一种文化的、集体的以及社会共有的财富得到珍视，我们就可以创造一个不害怕依赖性，不将依赖性妖魔化的社会；我们可以创造一个世界，在那里，有幸福的父母和稳定的童年，没有孩子会被精准调校以换取成功；我们期待这样一个世界，当我们决定如何重新分配社会盈余时，娱乐性和需要它的环境将被优先考虑；我们期待这样一个世界，在那里，父母有足够多的时间和空间，在孩子刚出生的时候，就能够与婴儿亲密交流。

被捧上神坛的专业管理阶级

到了2019年，25岁以上的美国人中有超过1/3的人拥有学士学位，这创下了当时历史上的最高纪录，使得学士学位证书成为进入专业管理阶级（PMC）的门槛。

大学，特别是一些小型文理学院的学生，他们通常会去学习语言认同的意义以及背后的附属政治关系。他们会去了解如何行使他们的社会权利，使得他们能够在自由职业领域发挥主导作用。另外，由于PMC的个性化、心理化和系统化，自由派领导人更容易忽视掉接近64%的没有获得学位的美国人，并且把他们视为落后群体和社会污点。

如果大多数美国人不上大学，那么私立文理学院的生源就会减少，公立大学承担了大部分的教育工作，但我们很少听到该类学校学生的个体事迹。他们是芸芸大众，是无名之辈，提起他们脑海中只能浮现出春假中的狂欢者或穿着七叶树服饰的足球迷的形象。在媒体舆论和大众印象中，小型文理学院的学生更优秀，尽管有时他们比其他同龄人更娇生惯养。文理学院是PMC精英诞生的摇篮，学生受到的教育格外重要。

自由派对普罗大众的不屑和媒体对精英私立院校的追捧影响了人们对史密斯学院事件的报道。史密斯学院是一所拥有近150年历史的女子学校，却因对媒体、阶级和种族之间的冲突处理不当而陷入困境。2018年7月，在史密斯学院校园，安保人员询问一名女学生为何会出现在本应关闭的楼栋内后，该名学生指控工作人员是种族主义者。

在社交媒体上，她公开指控了通风报信的看门人和两名与此事件无关的安保人员，并将他们称为种族主义者。她只是在正常用餐，却遭受了种族歧视的事引起了全国媒体的关注，史密斯学院的行政人员承诺会迅速采取行动来打击校园内的种族主义行为。

出乎意料的是，由该学院委托进行的独立调查没有发现被指控的工作人员有不当行为或种族偏见的证据。然而，大学管理部门仍然强迫调查人员参与暗示他们有罪的恢复性程序。在围绕该事件展开的关于种族问题的公共讨论背后潜藏着另一个关于阶级特权和社会经济弱势的故事。

捉摸不透的文理学院

2018年的史密斯学院事件是位于东北部农村地区其他私立院校情况的缩影，例如哈弗福德学院、阿默斯特学院、威廉姆斯学院和韦尔斯利学院。这些学院已成为PMC文化的实验室，吸引了来自私立高中和公立高中受过良好教育的学生。与竞争对手一样，史密斯学院一直在努力使其学生群体和老师群体多样化。史密斯学院试图在殖民时期的建筑中和常春藤覆盖的墙壁后营造其公平、多样和包容的理想氛围。但它的地理位置本身使这种努力毫无意义。

史密斯学院和许多其他文理学院一样，已经成为一个世界化、多样化的地方，它所在的马萨诸塞州和美国大部分农村一样遭受了数十年的经济停滞。2019年，北安普敦的失业率是波士顿的两倍，其经济依赖旅游业和教育业。像其他学院一样，史密斯学院雇蓝领与工会工人来清洁、维修他们的校园设施，或者在食堂为学生提供食物。

史密斯学院从当地招聘了较低级别的行政工作人员，以保证其官僚机构的顺利运作。对大学资源的良好管理意味着需要尽可能少地支付这类工人的工资，同时最大限度地将资金用于奖励知名教授和高层管理人员。不幸的是，对于大学的管理层来说，他们无法对工薪阶层员工进行有效管理。工薪阶层与PMC和崇拜PMC的学生团体不同，他们经常被自身的阶层所束缚。工薪阶层常被出生地所束缚，扎根于社区和家庭使他们只能靠绵薄的工资生存。

尽管美国的大学入学率不断提高，但是其经济流动性在过去50年中一直不好。高等教育的负担日益加重，几代美国大学生在背着学生贷款的情况下工作。受过教育的民众是社会的公共财富，也是实现民主的必要条件。然而，大学教育的普及并没有显著提高美国公共领域讨论的质量，而是夹在两极之间。一方面，像福克斯新闻这样的右翼媒体持续和阴谋论思想眉来眼去，贩卖愤怒、怀疑和仇外心理，而另一方面，像微软全国广播公司和美国有线电视新闻网这样的媒体在道德恐慌和PMC美德中摇摆不定。

我们甚至可以说，经济不平等的加剧和大学入学率的升高共同造就了一个分裂且多疑的政体。在实施精英统治及其世俗的自由主义道德准则背景下，不平等的经济体系加剧了贫富差距。为了满足自己的物质和精神需求，PMC精英们重新定义了自由主义道德准则。将教育当作跨越社会阶层的途径只是白日做梦，只会让腐败的精英统治体制继续苟延残喘而已。人们普遍认为，精英统治体制存在致命缺陷，不适合承担分配资源的任务。

在教育水平提高的同时，教育资源的分配越来越不平等，人们越来越想进入顶尖大学。私立学院的学位证书作为一个不可磨灭的标志性物品，将会伴随毕业生的一生。在拥有大学学位的美国人中，4%的人就读于私立文理学院。总的来说，小型文理学院的学生和毕业生约占所有美国人的1%至1.5%。即使在高等教育这个领域，声望和资本的差异也让富裕和贫穷的学院之间有了无情的鸿沟。在新冠疫情肆虐和股市高涨时期，史密斯学院已经预见它将会收到大额捐款，而相对贫穷的伊萨卡学院却要解雇20%的教职员工。

理想与现实

史密斯、阿默斯特和威廉姆斯等学院的学生可能并不都来自全国最富有的1%的人口，但他们是大学学生中非常特殊的一部分。在美丽的乡村环境中，他们受到同样是名校毕业生的教授们的密切关注。学生远离了来自家庭、就业和社会的压力，在小班教学中接受了全面教育，这种教育能让他们保持怀疑态度，能激发他们的好奇心，能培养他们的批判性思维，能让他们熟悉生活常识。这种苏格拉底式的教学，通过讨论、问答甚至辩论的方法，使得学生之间，以及学生和校友之间的关系愈发深厚。为了获得这些好处，雄心勃勃的学生和他们的家人不会对天价学杂费犹豫不决，史密斯学院每年的学杂费将近8万美元。它吹嘘其58%的学生都享受经济资助，可为什么不干脆降低学费呢？精英私立教育已成为一种奢侈品，一个慈善活动的重要场所。正如爱马仕包或古驰外套等奢侈品的价格不会下降一样。私立大学玩的是高定价再打折扣的把戏，发达资本主义虚假交易中的消费者对此再熟悉不过了。"支持"有价值的学生是一项慈善活动，学院的发展主任可以向富有的捐助者兜售可减税捐赠。

当然，在文理教育理想背后阴魂不散的史密斯校友实际上是种族主义者和帝国主义者。史密斯校友南希·里根为毒品战争发起了"坚决说不"（Just Say No）的宣传活动，而她的丈夫罗纳德·里根则缩小了"福利国家"规模，放松了对美国媒体的管制，削弱了工会权力，妖魔化了工人阶级中的非裔美国人，并忽视了艾滋病的流行。

在COVID-19病毒流行之前，像史密斯学院这样的大学收到的入学申请不断增加，在2018年达到了历史新高，有5,780名申请者。2020年，史密斯学院的捐赠达到19亿美元，即每人638,000美元。2020年10月，该学院收到了一笔金额最大的捐款：5,000万美元。这些数字是耶鲁大学毕业的校长凯瑟琳·麦卡特尼（Kathleen McCartney）成功的体现，她于2013年辞去了哈佛大学教育研究生院院长的职位，担任该学院的校长职务。根据最新的《高等教育纪事报》数据，麦卡特尼的高管薪酬总额为每年720,690美元。

尽管麦卡特尼有着心理学博士学位和杰出的学术生涯，但她和大多数当代大学领导人一样，一心想着筹款。她还紧随国家趋势，致力于重塑史密斯学院的文科大业，既是为了适应学生更务实的专业需求，也是为了满足创业文化迎合美国高等教育学术使命的需要。意料之中，在麦卡特尼的学院的网页上，她宣称她对创新、创业精神十分重视，并认为它们是学院教育的核心要素。她还致力于帮助学院的毕业生跻身企业高管。如今，46.7%的学院本科生主修数学和科学——在麦卡特尼的领导下，这一数字稳步上升。

如果麦卡特尼真的是在捍卫自由主义的教育理想、学术自由和专业研究方案，那她的理念就会与该校校董所代表的资本利益相冲突，与那些希望雇用雄心勃勃的毕业生的企业相矛盾。但现实恰恰相反，她和史密斯学院致力于提倡和培养领导力这一品质，并对此极力吹捧。我们不禁有些疑惑：学士学位本质上等同于新的工商管理硕士（MBA）吗？专业管理阶级的大学管理层与富有的校董和商业领袖已经狼狈为奸，他们的语言、发展前景和机构宗旨早已暗中挂钩，简而言之，他们是一个利益共同体。

"领导力"作为高等教育所提倡的一种品质，仅仅是满足商业需求的一个代号而已——如果我们思考一下文学和历史中著名领导者的品质，就会发现一系列与新自由主义制度极不相容的特征。冷酷无情、权欲熏心、领袖气质、不择手段、自我牺牲、坚忍克己、敏感多疑、果敢决绝、诡诈狡猾和一心一意都是真实或虚构的领导人所共有的品质，从拿破仑和凯瑟琳大帝到奥德修斯和恺撒大帝，再到圣女贞德、安德鲁·卡内基和亚伯拉罕·林肯，皆是如此。

当学校管理者谈到领导力是他们想传授给学生的一种价值观时，他们更有可能指的是使得通用电气公司裁员的首席执行官杰克·韦尔奇的例子，或失败的创业公司Theranos的创始人伊丽莎白·霍尔姆斯的例子，这位年轻女子说服投资者们相信她发明了一种革命性的方法，可以用非常少的血样快速进行血液检测。就像WeWork公司被罢免的CEO亚当·诺伊曼一样，她的领导素质和欺骗能力使她攫取了数亿乃至数十亿的财富。

新体制

像史密斯学院这样的高校，它也曾有虽不完美但非由资本主导的文科理想，当它完全屈服于企业管理层的要求时，该怎么做呢？

史密斯学院采用了一种充满社会正义、包容性、多样性和公平性的措辞，就算是摩根士丹利金融公司、花旗银行或埃克森美孚石油公司的HR都挑不出毛病。如果说觉醒前工作场所充满了性别歧视、种族主义和公开惩罚机制，鼓励提拔熟练运用计算机的男性白人员工，那么当代的工作场所已经演变成了一个监视和再培训的实验场所，所有这些都打着洗刷雇主罪名的幌子。

凯瑟琳·麦卡特尼对2018年涉嫌种族形象定性事件的处理被戏剧化地呈现了出来。事件发生后，史密斯学院对平均工资为43,000美元的员工进行了强制性反种族主义培训，并改建了友好宿舍以供"有色人种学生和黑人学生"居住。在摆脱工作场所的偏见或骚扰方面，尽管员工培训一再被证明是无效的，但美国各地的雇主都在投资这种针对性骚扰和种族主义的培训，以处理法律问题和责任问题，同时也作为摆脱偏见的象征。40年前，联邦政府就强制取消了公立学校和住房的种族隔离政策。40年后的今天，史密斯学院的管理层为有色人种学生划分了住宿范围，这等于变相承认了自己营造了一个种族对立的环境，使有色人种学生不得不通过单独居住来保护自己免受伤害。

同时，在教室里乃至整个校园，学生们感受到了一种非同寻常的特权文化，不仅在经济上，心理上也是如此。他们的每一个需求都得到了满足，他们的每一个想法都得到了教授的认可，教授们听从学生的召唤——以至于终身职位要由学生对教授"表现"的评价来决定。在这种文化中，社会正义的言论无处不在，但区分轻视、忧虑和真正的社会压迫的能力却正被悄然扼杀。而这些精英学院的前几代学生早已融入了社会，在统治阶级中占有一席之地。如今的学生用自我肯定、赋能和正义的言论作遮羞布，实际上却是为了攫取特权。新兴的精英阶层在攀登PMC的阶梯过程中，将"社会正义"发挥得淋漓尽致。

2018年7月31日的种族定性事件将大学文化中关于种族歧视的方面——暴露出来。自史密斯学院的大二学生卡努特在她的Facebook账号上揭露此事后，包括CNN、《纽约时报》和《华盛顿邮报》在内的全国性新闻媒体都就此进行了报道，报道中媒体强调了卡努特的心理创伤。在她的Facebook帖子中，卡努特说，当有人打电话给校园安保人员时，她正在史密斯学院的泰勒楼的生活区放松地吃着午饭。她描述说，在安保人员到来之前，她被一男一女监视着，他们在离她很远的一个房间里来回踱步，她因为自己的存在而感到焦虑。

当一名校园安保人员终于赶到，并在一名看门人的陪同下走近她后，二人质问卡努特是否有权利待在那里。

报道说，事件发生后卡努特受到了严重的心理创伤，她害怕在自己的房间里睡觉，无法恢复正常的校园生活。

卡努特说："我生来就是黑人。有些人质疑我为何在史密斯学院，这很令人气愤……任何有色人种学生都不应该被要求解释他们为什么在这所白人名校内。我尽了最大努力进入史密斯，我有权利安全地生活在我的校园里。"

作为对Facebook帖子的回应，麦卡特尼向卡努特公开道歉，并迅速对参与该事件的看门人作停职处理。报道中没有人对麦卡特尼的道歉或该工作人员的停职提出任何疑问。

卡努特本人在社交媒体的帖子中称那个看门人是"种族主义混混"。《华盛顿邮报》援引警务公平中心主席菲利普·阿提巴·戈夫的话说:"问题是,对许多人来说,执法部门已被视为他们的种族主义随从。"该描述暗示,史密斯学院看门人像一个执掌大权的贵族或老板,呼吁警察按照他的种族主义观点来管理校园。这个故事似乎证实了自由主义者对工薪阶级白人的猜测,他们倾向于毒害社会、传播根深蒂固的种族主义、散布恐惧和怨恨。那些在小型文科学院从事低薪工作的人也是如此——这些人缺乏主见,易受外界种族主义倾向的影响,以至于他们愿意以他们的生计为代价,为所谓的白人至上主义采取行动。

事件调查

如前所述,该事件仍有后续。

史密斯学院于2018年7月31日委托第三方对该事件进行了独立调查。调查报告显示,没有发现任何史密斯员工有不当行为的证据。调查报告在10月份被公开发表,记者艾玛·惠特福德在美国高等教育媒体上对其进行了报道,但仍没有引起主流媒体的关注。惠特福德报道称:史密斯学院委托了一家法律事务所对该员工进行调查,但没有任何证据表明其所作所为是出于种族歧视。该调查结果受到了众多校友及学生的质疑,而美国公民自由联盟也力挺黑人学生,谴责了该调查结果。

在联盟成员的见证下,调查员采访了匿名的"报警者"和餐厅的员工杰基·布莱尔,该员工在事发前曾为卡努特提供食物并与其有过短暂交流。该报告公开了两人之间的对话内容,以及卡努特、看门人、保安人员之间的对话内容。那位看门人,也就是报警人,是个60多岁的老人,这位老人在报警时犯了个错误:他完全可以在报警之前来和卡努特谈谈。但好在,该警员并未如卡努特所言携带了武器，在询问过程中，他对卡努特也极为礼貌，发现是误会后也表达了歉意。

2021年2月，《纽约时报》发表了迈克尔·鲍威尔对该事件的长篇调查。保守派以卡努特在Facebook中提到的两人为代表，描述了在该事件中工人阶级所处的困境。布雷特·斯蒂斯芬则在《纽约时报》的评论区内指责自由左派屈服于新左派。2021年3月，1776委员会的非裔领导人给史密斯学院写了一封公开信，谴责麦卡特尼对该事件处理不当。

> 我们中的许多人都是民权运动中的一员，坚决维护程序公正和无罪推定的原则，为获取法律上的平等待遇而战。我们的行动是为了保护所有族裔的美国人不被随意定罪；在雇佣他们的精英机构因畏惧媒体言论而裹足不前时，为他们提供支持，令他们免受流言蜚语的迫害；不让有特权的黑人根据"生活经验"随意控诉白人。

麦卡特尼向学生致歉时曾说她接受卡努特基于"生活经验"所作的控诉。

作为一名边缘人员，或者说一个小角色，史密斯学院的前员工乔迪·肖在媒体上引起了一场小规模的骚动。2018年7月的事件发生后，她拒绝在强制性的反偏见培训中谈论种族问题，然后辞去了学院的管理工作，并公开谴责史密斯学院内充斥着对白人员工的敌意。

她获得了右翼分子的支持，并在保守派的煽动者巴里·维斯的Substack平台上发表了致凯瑟琳·麦卡特尼的公开信，并在YouTube平台上表达了希望"变革"的"宏伟愿景"。肖，一个拥有两个孩子的单身母亲，已在知名众筹平台GoFundMe上筹集了20多万美元。她将自己视为史密斯学院员工的代言人，为那些不敢大声反抗麦卡特尼的管理的员工发声。作为史密斯学院的校友，肖在辞职时年薪仅为45,000美元，但即使她抵制了学院反偏见培训的思想侵蚀，却也并未成为工人阶级的英雄。她的YouTube视频和公开文字中充斥着白人工薪阶层独有的关于知名度、社会变革、受害者身份和代表性的陈词滥调。

同麦卡特尼一样，肖希望社会公众能够相信她的所作所为是为了维护学院白人员工的权利，她希望受到压迫的员工们能够大胆发声。尽管她看起来有些痴心妄想，但麦卡特尼的说法同样牵强，我们也应该对其进行严厉批判。麦卡特尼在致歉时断言学生有权出现在"史密斯学院的任何地方"，她声称管理部门将建立"一个包容、多样、可持续发展的校园……"。史密斯学院的所有成员都有责任确保每个人的安全，每个人都应得到尊重。因一名学生在Facebook上的帖子，麦卡特尼免去了门卫的工作，现实中雇主与雇员之间的不平等关系使麦卡特尼的行为带上了敌对色彩，而为了摆脱这种关系，麦卡特尼在文中反复强调"共同体"这个词。

麦卡特尼或许已展现出了必要的领导能力：作为一名崇尚新自由主义的领导，为展现对黑人群体的善意，她愿意在没有证据的情况下直接降罪于她的员工，又希望她的同事和学生们能够把她视作一名反种族主义社会的开明校长。仅仅是因为一名学生表达了不满，她便愿意在反种族主义斗争中牺牲工人，这是其固有阶级身份所展现出的又一标志性特征。我在其他部分曾表明，PMC精英们有一个陋习，那就是将贫穷的白人当作种族主义社会中罪孽的替罪羊。

自由主义者曾吹捧无罪推定原则和普遍怀疑论，并借此标榜自己的优越性，尤其是在与备受其唾弃的对手做比较时，例如苏联。当今的PMC领导人热衷于宣扬一种极为荒谬且反社会的道德模式，在面对缺乏判断和真实性的证据时，他们无视正当程序和理性，以自我美化的方式粉饰太平。我并不指望一所小型文科类学院的校长是社会主义者，或是进步人士，但对麦卡特尼与史密斯学院所捍卫的正当程序和事实认定原则完全相悖的行为，我的确感到十分震惊。

乔迪·肖现在依靠着其知名度和对史密斯学院的诉讼案件维持生计。麦卡特尼在新冠疫情流行期间被减了薪，但这种滥用职权的行为和之前错误的裁决并没有对她造成多大困扰，她仍旧稳当地坐在校长的职位上。麦卡特尼的行为表明了她对精英阶层的维护，即那些受教育程度最高、收入最高的人可以在摒弃现实真理的情况下，支配并胁迫那些被称作"社会成员"的下属。

不要让有钱的学生举报你

马克·帕特纳德是卡努特在Facebook中提到的被误认为是报警人的两名员工之一。他告诉《纽约时报》的记者："我们曾开玩笑说，不要让一个有钱的学生举报你，不然，你就会被开除。"关于2018年的事件，在有关史密斯学院员工、学生、行政部门三者关系的讨论中，这个笑话是为数不多的正确言论。在制造业的工作岗位从美国经济发达的新英格兰地区消失的同时，后工业时代的服务工作岗位正在增加，女性劳动者支持职业自由和文化产业的发展，她们逐渐成为维持美国名望经济（借用名望谋取利益的经济模式）的重要支柱。在后工业化的工作环境下，服务是关键，工人纪律依赖于顾客与技术的不断监管。

虽然卡尔·马克思将工厂描述成工人被剥削和胁迫的地狱，但从一键式购物到无人干预的文理教育，后工业化的工作环境应该是无冲突、无压迫的。劳动剥削者，这一最原始的称呼，逐渐被美化，被称作"觉醒"的管理层。如果说麦卡特尼和卡努特的战线是统一的，是因为她们都把史密斯学院最受尊重但工资最低的工人当作罪人，并对他们进行惩戒。

社会学家阿莉·拉塞尔·霍克希尔德在《心灵的整饰》一书中以空乘人员和收银员为研究对象，分析了他们的情绪管理方式。她强调说，正确的情感表达是后工业化服务工作中的一个关键要素。帕特纳德描述了这样一种情况：史密斯学院餐厅的员工或清洁工不仅要做好本职工作，还必须对学生有良好的服务态度，否则就有可能被指责和解雇。

卡努特提到的餐厅工作人员布莱尔是史密斯学院的雇员。布莱尔当天在泰勒餐厅服务。她与卡努特进行了简短的交流，介绍了餐厅在夏季的进出制度，即餐厅在夏季时已被参加夏令营的青少年预订。所有打给校园警察的电话都有记录，因此可以证明布莱尔确实没有报警，而帕特纳德在打电话的时候也的确没有在工作。

在卡努特的帖子发布后，布莱尔被误认作报警人，她在家里接到电话，被咒骂"不配活着"，在车上发现贴着的纸条：指责她是一个种族主义者。即使她没有任何不当行为，但学院管理层仍施压，要求布莱尔与卡努特进行调解。布莱尔拒绝了。在2018年8月史密斯学院的公告中，麦卡特尼在提到该事件时，提出了"恢复正义……愿意道歉、宽恕与和解"的想法。使用一个与司法相关的术语以及要求布莱尔参加调解，麦卡特尼暗示布莱尔已经犯了罪。但在接下来的几个月内，独立调查报告的发表证明了布莱尔无罪。

隐性的伤害

史密斯学院的所有员工现在都必须参加反种族主义的培训，培训要求白人员工谈论他们童年的种族经历，同时"坦白"自己怀有种族主义思想。如果说马克思所研究的资本家在19世纪是想要从工人身上榨取尽可能多的体力价值，那么后工业时代的领导们似乎是想要洗脑员工，侵蚀和重塑工人的思想。那么对种族公正的要求是如何演变成一种新的员工纪律的？

一个可能的原因是，PMC的领导们一直渴望找到能够将员工分门别类的方法，鼓励有关偏见的对话，从而转移员工们对职场中残酷的阶级斗争和权力斗争的注意力。鲍威尔在《纽约时报》的报道中引用了史密斯学院里一位教授的一句话："可以肯定地说，在史密斯学院里，种族问题比阶级问题要被讨论得更多。这是精英学术机构的一个特点，教师和学生都没有意识到成为精英意味着什么。"

PMC的精英们已经知道，他们可以利用所谓的白人工薪阶层的种族主义来为美国资本主义社会分层和经济不平等辩护。否则，史密斯学院这所自称专注于社会公正的学校，怎么能让大家相信校长和普通员工之间存在的巨大薪资差异是合理的呢？

1972年，理查德·森内特和乔纳森·科布出版了《阶级的隐性伤害》一书，汇总了对150名工薪阶层白人的采访结果。这些人住在波士顿被两位作者称为"城中村"的地方，距离北安普顿大学和史密斯学院只有几个小时的车程。森内特和科布把注意力集中在对弗兰克·里沙罗（化名）的采访上，在采访中，里沙罗以忏悔的方式对他们说了3个小时，一句话也没停过。里沙罗出身贫寒，在父亲的虐待下长大，努力在银行找到了一份底层的白领工作。作者称："里沙罗以一种独特的方式与采访者交谈：他把采访者当作拥有更高地位、受过更高等教育、有着与自己截然不同的生活方式的救赎者，他在采访者面前为自己的一生辩护。"

里沙罗尤其为自己无法掌控自己的生活，无法在工作中获得自主权和满足感而感到羞愧。他认为，接受过大学教育的面试官在工作中享有一种他所没有的尊严。虽然他对那些接受过大学教育、对待工作非常放松、从不参与体力劳动的同事表现出一种随意的蔑视，但其实面对比他受教育程度更高的人他内心产生了一种自卑感。

森内特和科布平等地对待里沙罗，由于他们表现出的同理心，里沙罗能够开诚布公地向他们讲述自己的生活。但是，这也恰恰证明了森内特和科布是PMC成员中的例外。接受过大学教育的精英们越来越不愿意面对像里沙罗这样的人，放弃把阶级纳入分析的范畴，而更倾向于任何其他形式的差异。大学已经开始用更友好的术语"第一代"来给工薪阶层的学生分类，校方相信，大学教育将使学生从原生家庭中脱颖而出，因此他们的后代今后也将继续接受大学教育。

在森内特和科布的研究项目已经过去50年之后的今天，史密斯学院的麦卡特尼已经证明，里沙罗对受过大学教育的精英采取防御态度是非常正确的。森内特和科布对里沙罗的痛苦感到惊讶：他逃离了一个暴力的工薪阶层家庭，得到了一份较低层次的白领工作，但他依然受缚于工作的空虚和徒劳。由于无法适应不停发展的社会文化，里沙罗始终无法定位自己的社会角色。森内特和科布对波士顿地区的白人工薪阶层的世界很感兴趣：这个世界的人们联系紧密，但孤立于外界。这里的居民觉得有必要证明自己值得获得尊重。受过大学教育的人享有的尊严是工薪阶层认为自己必须不断努力才能争取到的。这种自发的防御性以及阶级社会随意评判他们所带来的伤害，迫使他们加入彼此紧密联系的社区，但他们的后代最终会反抗这一现实。

在《阶级的隐性伤害》出版两年后，波士顿校车骚乱在工薪阶层的白人社区爆发，州政府被迫将该区的公立学校整合。白人工薪阶层对坐大巴进入白人社区的黑人学生施暴的丑陋画面深深烙进了PMC自由主义者的心里。有钱的白人家庭纷纷搬出波士顿这个城中村，要么搬到郊区，要么把孩子送到当地更优秀的私立学校就读。森内特和科布选择白人族群聚居地作为他们的社会学研究地点，这里与PMC的自由主义世界的疏远程度越来越高，许多工薪阶层白人退回到他们自己的郊区，以罗纳德·里根总统保守的反新政政治作掩护。

布朗诉教育局案（Brown v. Board of Education）是美国最高法院审理的案件，它促成了美国公立学校系统的种族融合，它对教育资源和学生人数平等的坚持却在今天成为模糊的记忆。在我们这个时代，大学管理者极力吹捧管理形式的多样性和包容性，但平等性几乎从未被提及。实际上的种族隔离，就像史密斯学院实行的友好宿舍制度，代表了一种新的身份碎片化。

自20世纪70年代初以来，美国的每一个民族、每一个种族、每一个收入阶层间的不平等都在加剧：从非裔美国人到亚裔美国人，再到全社会的收入分配，财富越来越集中到每个处在群体顶端的人手中，迫使处于中间和底层的人在工资缩水、生活质量下降和工作条件恶化的状况下挣扎着生存。

正是在这个国家经济不平等日益加剧的荒谬背景下，卡努特在史密斯学院所经历的真正恐惧促使麦卡特尼判定她的员工犯了美国种族歧视罪。尤其是2008年金融危机之后，新经济和全球化的光芒可能已经褪去，阶层分化仍在加剧。对工人阶级和所有劳工的诋毁，使得PMC能够掌控这样一种局面，即它仅仅服务于资本的心血来潮，却披着自以为是的华丽外衣。由于无法超越自身利益，它把社会正义变成了个人的事情，只能由个人处理。在后工业经济中，工人阶级必须放下自尊，才能适应为PMC服务。

在史密斯学院，工人必须把自己隐形，才能满足自己对社会公正制度的幻想，而这只是为了让学生们享受到没有冲突、一帆风顺的大学生活。卡努特不是种族主义的受害者，而是PMC利用种族和贫穷问题指导的反社会活动的受害者。她了解，只要在Facebook上发帖抱怨，她就能诱使大学校长道歉，并让美国公民自由联盟（ACLU）迅速为她辩护。这对任何青少年来说都不是一个很好的示例：仅仅说出自己的怀疑就可能会导致一个人的生计被不明不白地摧毁。为那些被冤枉的员工洗刷冤屈的调查，将永远把卡努特的名字与一场由大学"领导"精心策划的闹剧联系在一起。这位"领导"是一位经验丰富、受过良好教育的女性，她本应更加慎重地对待自己的学生和员工。

2018年史密斯学院发生的事件揭露了一个事实：在一个社会安全网严重破损的世界里，精英阶层试图压制对工薪阶层就业状况的探讨。在没有国家医保的情况下，失业对任何工人来说都是灾难。麦卡特尼可以通过扭曲校园政治和社会正义的观念来误导我们，以掩饰自己利用高层身份滥用权力的事实，但我们应该扪心自问，做出这种行为的人竟能逃脱惩罚，那她教出来的学生会接受良好教育吗？除此之外，我们还应该问问自己：史密斯学院和其他类似的学院是否应该存在？私立大学在把自己建设成一个虚幻的无阶级社区的过程中发挥了什么样的社会作用？这些大学无脑吹捧美国的创新、创业精神，贯彻为达目的不择手段的思想，而不是追求真正的教育和切实的公平正义。

现在是时候考虑解散私立大学及其捐赠基金会，并将它们与公立机构合并了，就史密斯学院，它附近有公立大学，如马萨诸塞大学阿默斯特分校（University of Massachusetts Amherst）。该校有24,233名本科生，其中77%的学生来自当地。经过几十年的财政紧缩政策，该校的学费却一直在稳步上涨，但本地学生的学费（15,791美元）仍然不到史密斯学院学费（55,830.31美元）的三分之一。马萨诸塞大学阿默斯特分校已经是麻省五校联盟之一，该联盟还包括汉普郡学院、史密斯学院、芒特霍利奥克学院和阿默斯特学院，学生被允许在这些学院中自由选择学习的课程。

如果实现结构平等是自由主义的目标之一，那么废除私立大学捐赠基金会应该是国家必须考虑的第一步。伯尼·桑德斯提议，为全民提供免费的公立高等教育，但这依然没有缩小公立大学、社区大学和精英私立大学之间的结构性差距。教育和财富已经被一个完全腐败的、谄媚于资本的阶级扭曲和囤积，现在是时候大胆想象一个完全不同的未来了，一个建立在解放公共利益以及教育和财富社会化基础上的未来。

受教育是每个人与生俱来的权利。经过50年的新自由主义教育，我们必须剥去美德的面纱，因为在这层面纱后面，是精英们试图隐藏的，他们对他们所统治的人民的深深蔑视。

结　　语

　　马克思所著的《资本论》适用于全世界。工人们在满是生产资料和生产工具的世界里，互相竞争与合作，一心一意扑在生产上，艰难地从金银矿铁、原木棉麻中提取价值与财富——在马克思眼里，如果这些工人敢于反抗资本主义，他们就拥有改变世界、创造历史的能力。PMC精英们也视自己为历史的创造者。他们在一个充斥着空洞符号、统计分析、推断预测、身份操演、道德高地、情感生产的世界里卖力工作。他们的爱情和生活都是虚无的、空洞的。即使在新冠疫情肆虐之时，他们的工作仍有增无减。在这种符号操纵的体制下的人们喜欢将愤怒作为激化道德恐慌的武器，但这些人不能也不愿意视自己为这个阶级的一员。在自由职业中，他们彼此监督，迫使在这个阶级中的所有人能够拥护和加强这个阶级的一致性——一种被要求在社会层面和知识层面的一致性，一种从根本上被竞争与个人主义割裂了的一致性。所有PMC批准了的有关种族主义和偏见歧视的政策都反过来加强了PMC成员的政治参与感与在文化上和道德上的优越感。在竞争激烈的市场环境中，他们或多或少都打破过自己曾经珍视的道德底线，转而一味地追求犯罪美学背后的刺激感，或者更甚，追求犯罪本身。

　　与冷漠老练，超级世故的外表截然不同，PMC精英们会在处理有关不平等的事件时感情用事，他们往往会一厢情愿地把自己当作受害者的"救世主"，向孤身一人的普通人施舍亟须的帮助。PMC急切想成为公平与正义的化身。在马克思看来，工业资本主义的先锋阶级会从这种独特的劳动过程中诞生。不幸的是，管理阶层人员和专业人士从来都不属于这个阶级，但是他们用坚忍不拔与审时适度等夸词来掩盖他们是资本主义的走狗的事实。而这种坚忍变通的精神，在PMC精英们的世界观里，恰恰是工人阶级所缺少的。是工人们创造了今天的世界，但今天PMC精英们憎恨这股来自过去的激烈的革命力量。精英们渴望掌控社会的变化，即使他们的分内之事都被统治阶级代表的意识形态牢牢限制。尽管他们知道自己所做的一切都是徒劳的，但他们仍然不愿相信若要重塑经济体系，就必须要让统治阶级做出改变。而这种改变的结果正好符合这群"救世主"的目标——让更多的普通人找到更好的工作，在经济上有更多保障，过上既有尊严又有意义的生活。

在研究PMC投资历史反映出的意识形态时，我并不只是想简单地"理解"PMC的概念以扩充知识宝库，恰恰相反，我感兴趣的是如何批评它的价值观，来帮助我对抗PMC宣扬的政治理念。为了建成社会主义的未来，我们必须不断斗争，不断克服因为中心主义和伪激进主义导致的政治瘫痪。纵观世界，学历在本科以下的普通人往往拒绝接受PMC所代表的专家治国论，他们更加偏向于支持民粹主义和极权主义，因为他们不再接受当权新自由主义者宣传的"有限的资源应通过竞争分配"这一套。在大多数没有受过大学教育的人眼里，PMC表现得越来越迂腐和虚伪，越来越残忍和脱离大众：在专权主义社会中，保守派永远是科学界最不能容忍的一类人，因此这群老古董也终于认清了自己是多么无能、狂怒和无知无助。在被煽动的人群里，他们终于发现自己的主权一直在被剥夺，他们四处发泄怒火。当然，这并不代表我会赞同他们，他们支持坐拥百万家财的民粹分子和他们的爪牙，这种行为在我看来是完全的反动派。但解决民粹主义的方案并不是什么自由改良主义和什么温和的中间派，而是社会主义。如果PMC始终坚持经济再分配必须由企业友好型"专家"掌管，社会主义者就不得不在构建新的政治秩序和计算新的政治参与成分上下功夫，这样做的目的是在社会主义光辉照不到的阴影下建立团结坚固的统一战线。

亲爱的读者，你或许和我一样，是PMC中的一员，或至少在PMC承办的机构里接受过教育。我希望我对这个阶级虚假性的简短介绍能让你认识到这个阶级里都是些自说自话、自夸自大的政治演员，同时让你在批判这个反动阶级的基础上坚定拒绝PMC宣扬的政治的决心。我们必须认识到我们一直被PMC精英们灌输着他们宣扬的精神思想和意识形态，我们必须尽已所能消除这种影响，从下而上自发地加入这场阶级斗争。这本小册子可以作为我们识别自己是否隶属于PMC或受PMC的价值观多大影响的指南，并且帮助我们更好地清算这个阶级。由于PMC价值观的参与扭曲了左派政党的意识形态，一切政治参与都必须以自我批评开始。我们必须摆脱PMC希望我们对成功、知识、种族、暴力、儿童、阅读、医保和性的思考方式。我们必须拒绝把这个阶级的品位和消费习惯当作成功的必备"美德"。我们必须明白我们是被资本主义不断剥削的受害者。我知道想要做到这些并不容易，因为PMC精英们已经掌控了我们生活的方方面面，如果我们不遵循他们畏缩的政治守则，我们就会在不知不觉中被他们排除在外，生活得更加艰难。

PMC会让我们忘记它是一个阶级，是一个利益至上的阶级，是一个为资本主义服务的阶级。然而不幸的是，PMC在垄断进步思想和开明政治方面如鱼得水，即使这个阶级已经放弃了自由主义者所珍视的专业精神和能让思想自由发展的民主文化。专业主义的价值观、大公无私的问责制度和尊重真理的研究团体是建设社会主义的关键。专业主义不是统一战线的敌人。专业主义中的专业精神及其严格的纪律性是培养社会主义专家的必要条件。优秀的社会主义专家是监督大规模的经济再分配和加强公共基础设施、提供更好的公共产品的主心骨，这对于地球资源的可持续发展和民主政治的存续是必不可少的。

我是在新冠疫情期间完成的这本小册子。这场疫情无论是经济上还是公共卫生上都对美国造成了空前的灾难，这与营利性医疗保健集团和已经空心化的公共卫生服务产业有着直接的关联。拜登·哈里斯政府反对全民医疗保险就很能说明问题。中间派的专家们对此事视而不见，反而将矛头指向个人行为，比如极力倡导戴口罩，并将之当作一种新时代的"美德"。没错，我们是应该戴口罩，但我们更应该做的是要求政府提供免费的核酸检测、行程追踪服务和疫苗，同时重建公共卫生秩序，为人民服务，而不是一切以利益为主。如果时光倒流，一切回归正常，你的老板或医保公司的推销员试图把你的健康商品化，作为一种"健康"协议推销给你时，请记住，医疗保健是公共基础设施的一部分，它并不是商品。正如为每个家庭提供优质保育应该被包含在公共基础设施中一样，为老弱病残提供保障应该成为最首要的投资目标。我的目标很简单：帮助社会主义经济和政治正常化。社会主义本身是朴实无华的：它不会用流行的代词或花哨的新词喧宾夺主。其符号不是空洞虚无的：它的政策与可靠的数据、客观的现实以及科学的方法紧密结合。社会主义工作者要拒绝披着博学、超凡脱俗的外衣高高在上，而应深入群众，与工人和被剥削者们统一起来做阶级斗争。PMC中无论是保守派还是进步派的精英们和他们所控制的机构都对工人阶级和社会主义本身有着极深的敌意。因此，为了打赢这场拉锯战，形成团结的统一战线比以往任何时候都要重要。尽管一时冲动的抗议活动、喧闹的人群和暴力的骚乱可能为社会变革带来一些政治上的契机，但这与我们所需要的程度、规模还远远不及。为了达到心中的目标，我们需要具备一种严格的纪律性，一种向来被左翼学术派不齿的纪律性。虽然混合经济是短期内我们可能达成的结果，但不妨让我们更进一步，在这种混合体系中注入更多社会主义力量。虽然PMC精英们极力推崇资本积累和他们所谓的"美德"，但我们必须摆脱他们对我们喜好和人际关系的清教徒式控制。我们即是异教徒，我们即是亵渎之人。

PMC精英们拒绝为现在糟糕的经济体系负责，也拒绝承认他们破坏了我们对公共机构的信任，毁坏了我们的公共卫生系统，损害了我们的童真，降低了我们的幸福感。PMC既不邪恶也不善良，它只是一个世俗功利的对手。在宣传资本主义是人民的敌人时，我们还必须指出敌人最勤勉的朝臣和最合格的马屁精是专业管理阶级（PMC）。

Introduction

FOR AS LONG as most of us can remember, the professional managerial class (PMC) has been fighting a class war, not against capitalists or capitalism, but against the working classes. Members of the PMC have memories of a time when they were more progressive—during the Progressive Era, specifically. They once supported working-class militancy in its epic struggles against robber barons and capitalists like Mrs. Leland Stanford Jr., Andrew Carnegie, John D. Rockefeller, and Andrew Mellon, but today, they go to Stanford and view private foundations bearing those same names as models of philanthropy and sources of critical funding and recognition. They still believe themselves to be the heroes of history, fighting to defend innocent victims against their evil victimizers, but the working class is not a group they find worth saving, because by PMC standards, they do not behave properly: they are either disengaged politically or too angry to be civil. Liberal members of the credentialed classes love to use the word *empower* when they talk about "people," but the use of that verb objectifies the recipients of their help while implying that the people have no access to power without them. The PMC as a proxy for today's ruling class is shameless about hoarding all forms of secularized virtue: whenever it addresses a political and economic crisis produced by capitalism itself, the PMC reworks political struggles for policy change and redistribution into individual passion plays, focusing its efforts on individual acts of "giving back" or reified forms of self-transformation. It finds in its particular tastes and cultural proclivities the justification for its unshakable sense of superiority to ordinary working-class people. If its politics amount to little more than virtue signaling, it loves nothing more than moral panics to incite its members to ever more pointless forms of pseudo-politics and hypervigilance. The much-maligned Hillary Clinton was honest in her contempt for ordinary people when, in 2016, she dismissed Trump supporters as "deplorables." Their

2016 defiance of PMC and liberal nostra has only hardened into reactionary antiauthoritarianism, which another reactionary demagogue will seek to exploit. PMC virtue hoarding is the insult added to injury when white-collar managers, having downsized their blue-collar workforce, then disparage them for their bad taste in literature, bad diets, unstable families, and deplorable child-rearing habits.

When the PMC sympathized with the plight of masses of working people, it also pioneered professional standards of research grounded in professional organizations like the American Medical Association, the Association of University Professors, and all the professional organizations that currently dominate academic life. In organizing professional life, the PMC tried to protect the integrity of specialists and experts against the power of capitalists and the markets. From Jane Addams to John Dewey, members of the early American PMC established academic freedom and the role of research in guiding public policy as critical to the development of industrial democracy. In doing so, the first social workers, muckraking journalists and radical social scientists, were following the lead of American workers and the Socialist Party led by Eugene Debs in a millennial struggle for worker power. Those heady days of PMC heroism are long gone. The PMC, with its professional discipline and aura of disinterestedness, did very well for itself during the Depression, during World War II, and in the postwar period with the expansion of universities and the growing complexity of the American and social economic order. When the tide turned against American workers, the PMC preferred to fight culture wars against the classes below while currying the favor of capitalists it once despised. The culture war was always a proxy economic war, but the 1960s divided the country into the allegedly enlightened and the allegedly benighted, with the PMC able to separate itself from its economic inferiors in a way that seemed morally justifiable.

It was after 1968 that the PMC gradually shifted its allegiance from workers to capital. Since that time, the most successful and visible segments of the PMC have brazenly put their smarts at the service of the bosses. If Marx theorized that class struggle was the engine of historical change and the political agent of it the proletariat, the newest incarnation of the PMC tries to make history by undermining working-class power and ignoring working-class interests. The post-1968 PMC elite has become ideologically convinced of its own unassailable position as comprising the most advanced people the earth has ever seen. They have, in fact, made a virtue of their vanguardism. Drawing on the legacy of the counterculture and its commitment to technological and spiritual innovations, PMC elites try to tell the rest of us how to live, and in large part, they have succeeded in destroying and building in its own image the physical and now cybernetic infrastructure of our everyday lives. As the fortunes of the PMC elites rose, the class insisted on its ability to do ordinary things in extraordinary, fundamentally superior and more virtuous ways: as a class, it was reading books, raising children, eating food, staying healthy, and having sex as the most culturally and affectively advanced people in human history. While the conservative critique of this "new" class, whether from Herman Kahn, William F. Buckley, Newt Gingrich, or David Brooks and Tucker Carlson, is pure media theater, its condemnation of liberalism's secret contempt for ordinary people rings true. Right-wing pundits heard the rage of ordinary people, but they weaponized that feeling for reactionary political purposes. No one has been as effective at mobilizing popular resentment of the PMC as Donald Trump. He merely stepped in to take advantage of decades of successful conservative propaganda positioning PMC liberalism as the enemy of the people and popular interests. Trump never pretended to be virtuous: his id-driven politics and lack of self-control formed the core of his appeal to those who felt scorned by the liberal superego. To defeat reactionary politics masquerading as populism, we need anti-PMC class struggle from the Left, not more identity politics, which has become just another vehicle of PMC virtue signaling. The Democratic Party, however, is not the political organization that will lead us in a struggle against capitalism and its deeply destructive system of exploitation and rent seeking.

My brief introduction to the PMC is polemical: for a recent "objective" account of the term, one need look no further than Gabriel Winant's "Professional Managerial Chasm: a Sociological Designation Turned into an Epithet and Hurled Like a Missile," for *N+1*. Unlike Winant's article, the work represented here is not a neutral piece of professional scholarship, refining terms and their definitions, insisting on nuance, and then finger wagging at those on the Left who are allegedly uncivil, who cannot hold polite discussions, and who hurl epithets at their enemies like missiles. Winant believes in liberal virtue; I do not. Winant published his PMC apologia and his left-bashing article at a time when Elizabeth Warren was leading in the 2019 polls, before voting began in the Democratic primaries. Warren failed to place second or sometimes even third or fourth in all the states that voted. Winant urged Sanders's supporters to bend the knee and reconcile themselves to Warren's brand of progressive professionalism. He did not foresee that it was Sanders who would win primary after primary while voters resoundingly rejected Warren's brand of limited progressivism.

The reasons for this rejection are manifold, but centrists and liberals want to ignore popular distrust of incremental solutionism by dismissing the collective desire for radical economic reorganization. In the United States, generations of allegedly neutral experts have hollowed out public goods, degraded the public sphere, facilitated the monetization of everything from health to aptitude, and indebted generations of Americans in a fantasy of meritocracy enhanced social mobility. Liberals have sat by while finance capital and corporate interests gutted the public treasury. Winant, however, historicizes the PMC and asks us not to abandon its values. In criticizing the PMC by offering a polemical account of its morals, I hope to weaken its power over the way we think about politics. The endgame in my critique is a return to socialist politics and socialist policies, once marginalized by PMC thought leaders and made visible by the historic 2016 and 2020 presidential campaigns of Bernie Sanders. Now that we have seen the results of the 2020 Democratic primaries, however, I am even more sure that Warren and the rest of the PMC will be standing in the way of real political change. Angling for a place in the new Biden administration, Warren has proven herself more interested in her own professional ascendancy than in the political ideology and social values that she and Sanders are supposed to share.

According to John and Barbara Ehrenreich, the PMC is made up of "salaried mental workers who do not own the means of production and whose major function in the social division of labor may be described broadly as the reproduction of capitalist culture and capitalist class relations." While Siegfried Kracauer and C. Wright Mills described white-collar workers as clerks, salespeople, and office workers who were shielded from physical labor, the Ehrenreichs' PMC comprises de-racinated, credentialed professionals, such as culture industry creatives, journalists, software engineers, scientists, professors, doctors, bankers, and lawyers, who play important managerial roles in large organizations. During the 1960s, young members of the class saw Robert McNamara, prosecutor of the Vietnam War, as the clear enemy of progress: for them McNamara was a cold-blooded killer, but he was simply a very high level member of their class. Today's PMC may not wear pocket protectors, but it has overseen the devastation of the lives and livelihoods of poor and working-class Americans of all races, genders, and sexualities in the name of equality of opportunity, competitiveness, austerity, and efficiency. Since the 1970s, PMC elites have been happy to abandon mass politics to reproduce the social division of labor and the widening gulf between those who prosper under late capitalism and those who do not.

American conservatives have shown themselves more willing to talk about class antagonism than liberals like Winant. For instance, in an article called "The Real Class War," *American Affairs* editor Julius Krein described the current political situation in America as one shaped by class war between the 0.01 percent and the top 10 percent, or the PMC. For him, the American working class has been so beaten down that it has no political agency at all. For Krein, a better, more enlightened PMC has to emerge to reverse policies that have intensified inequality across every economic stratum. More militant than Winant, Krein urged PMC elites to act in their self-interest to fight against "intra-elite inequality: in order to help the immiserated working class to overthrow our own 'pathetic' oligarchs, the lower tiers of the PMC must lead the fight against alienation and exploitation." In the same issue of *American Affairs*, Krein published Amber Frost's "The Characterless Opportunism of the Managerial Class," a counterpoint article in which the author argues that the PMC is composed of unreliable, shape-shifting "rear guarders."

In 2019, Michael Lind published *The New Class War: Saving Democracy from the Managerial Elite*. In this book, Lind wants to resuscitate the American ideal of a classless society, and he blames the managerial elite for the rise of Anglo-American populism. I do not entirely disagree. Lind also denounces the PMC for its demonization of the working-class rejection of centrist incrementalism. Lind is that strangest of creatures, an antisocialist advocate for working-class power. As such, he is able to address the failings of Occupy Wall Street and its neglect of class conflict for anarchist proceduralism and the cultural turn that facilitated such politics, but his goal of securing a lasting class peace implies a neat, negotiated resolution to class antagonism that is managerial and administrative rather than political and objective. What terrifies Lind and most centrists, conservative and liberal, is the idea that really, implemented socialism, as a form of political governance, is not the end of class struggle but only its real beginning.

As a class, the PMC loves to talk about bias rather than inequality, racism rather than capitalism, visibility rather than exploitation. Tolerance for them is the highest secular virtue—but tolerance has almost no political or economic meaning. The Right is well aware of liberal preening, and it has weaponized popular resentment against this class of alleged hypocrites. Fox News lives to own liberals; reactionary hatred of professionals and professionalism come not out of love for the people but out of fealty to the special sovereignty of free markets to solve all social problems. In fact, conservatives need a functioning and powerful PMC cadre of inhibited professionals to serve as punching bags for their politics of popular resentment. The PMC continues to oblige these reactionaries by betraying popular policies like Medicare for All, opting instead for means-tested, think tank–brewed Big Pharma and lobbyist-approved forms of health care that allow for profit taking to take place at the expense of public health and health care workers. Insurance companies have doubled their profits since the beginning of the coronavirus pandemic. Their most powerful lobbyists have the Democratic Party in their thrall. It turns out that PMC virtue is also the color of money.

Although the PMC is profoundly secular in nature, its rhetorical tone is pseudo-religious. While the PMC infuriates conservative Christians with its media monopoly on liberal righteousness, it finds salvation, like most Protestant sects, in material and earthly success. In liberal circles, talking about class or class consciousness before other forms of difference is not just controversial; it is heretical. They call you a "class reductionist" if you argue that race, gender, and class are not interchangeable categories. They pile on with the legalistic and deadly term *intersectional* to accommodate the materialist critique of their politics. The PMC simply does not want its class identity or interests unmasked. Young people wanting to enter what the Ehrenreichs called the "liberal professions" and gain positions in academia and the culture and media industries have had to adapt themselves to the Procrustean bed of PMC-dominated networks of influence. Anyone who wants to privilege class critique should be prepared to be thoroughly red-baited and asked questions like "Why do you wear presentable clothes when you're a socialist? Shouldn't you wear burlap sacks?" and "Why do you enjoy sports? Isn't that part of the military–industrial complex?" and "Why do you encourage conflict? Aren't you irresponsibly fomenting violence?" PMC elites believe that asceticism is the fate of the leftist and that any kind of social conflict arising from corrosive inequality is her fault. In promoting these casual assumptions about leftism, the PMC defends capitalism as the purveyor of both luxury and harmony. Gabriel Winant's characterization of the Left's warlike language is just one example of liberalism's attempts to discipline its antagonist, the socialist who takes issue with the PMC. What leftists must accept is that for us, there is no class without class antagonism and class contradiction. I do not opine on the PMC because I hope to have a civil discussion about our differences: I am writing this critique to isolate the PMC's historically grounded, virtue-hoarding politics of liberal refusal to adopt and support the social and political changes we desperately need.

In 1977, the Ehrenreichs were the first to predict that PMC values and ideology would dominate liberal and eventually neoliberal politics for the foreseeable future. Since they published their essay, the class and its defining characteristics have evolved and morphed as its powers have expanded and capitalism has become even more predatory. In fact, the fungibility of the PMC is part of the class's structural dynamism. The Ehrenreichs' analysis allows us to isolate and identify the hegemony of a class that has, in its most recent incarnation, become desperate to hold on to the power it has accrued since the 1970s. The dark social consequences of its monopoly on expertise, in addition to its attempts to monopolize public virtue while blocking any attempts at meaningful economic redistribution, have given shape to our present political situation.

The Ehrenreichs drew from Siegfried Kracauer's study of interwar salaried masses in Berlin, who were the quintessentially deluded political subjects. They despised anyone who did physical labor and dreamed about instant luxury and wealth while enthusiastically writing their own pink slips. C. Wright Mills condemned the postwar white-collar worker as hopelessly identified with selling and thought of this particular worker as particularly susceptible to market discipline and its prefab, reified versions of personality and intersubjectivity. Christopher Lasch believed the white-collar, managerial classes to be hopelessly and collectively hypnotized by their own narcissism. For the Ehrenreichs, the contemporary PMC embodies all of these qualities identified by left social critics of the past, but the new elites of this class have weaponized their identification with capitalism. Even though they look down on the vulgarity and stupidity of the masses, they are entirely indifferent and even hostile to the professional protocols and norms defended by their liberal precursors. They actually hold in high value a tradition-and history-busting form of entrepreneurialism that courts publicity and hates hierarchy and organization.

Since you are reading this book, you are probably, like me, an ambivalent member of the PMC. I am at best a second-generation PMC person, but I do not like what I see of my class, and I am determined to fight to socialize the things that the PMC wants to hoard: virtue, grit, persistence, erudition, specialized knowledge, prestige, and pleasure, along with cultural and actual capital. To define the changing contours of a class to which one partially belongs is to enter into the difficult process of political self-criticism, beginning with an exfoliating and brutal reconceptualization and historicization of one's own values, sensibilities, and affects. To renounce one's narcissistic fetishization of intelligence or refinement is not a simple act. This short introduction aims at helping us do the necessary work of self-criticism while providing a few tools to attack PMC positions in its best-defended redoubts—political organizations, publishing, media, private foundations, think tanks, and the university.

While the Right represents an obdurate obstacle to economic reorganization and large-scale social redistribution, it is actually the liberal PMC that stands in the way of the political revolution necessary to forge a different kind of society and world, one in which the dignity of ordinary people and the working class takes center stage. The PMC is deeply hostile to simple redistributive policies that a Bernie Sanders presidency would have implemented: it is against the idea of building solidarity among the oppressed. It prefers obscurantism, balkanization, and management of interest groups to a transformative reimagination of the social order. It wants to play the virtuous social hero, but as a class, it is hopelessly reactionary. The interests of the PMC are now tied more than ever to its corporate overlords than to the struggles of the majority of Americans whose suffering is merely background décor for the PMC's elite volunteerism. Members of the PMC soften the sharpness of their guilt about collective suffering by stroking their credentials and telling themselves that they are better and more qualified to lead and guide than other people.

PMC centrism is a powerful ideology. Its priorities in research and innovation have been shaped more and more by corporate interests and the profit motive, while in the humanities and social sciences, scholars are rewarded by private foundations for their general disregard for historical knowledge, not to mention historical materialism. The rewards for following ruling-class directives are just too great, but the intellectual and psychic price that has to be paid for compliance should be too high for any member of society. In academia, the American PMC has achieved a great deal in establishing the rigors of peer review consensus and research autonomy, but we can no longer afford to defend its cherished principle of epistemological neutrality as a secret weapon against "extremism." We live in a political, environmental, and social emergency: class war over distribution of resources is the critical battle of our times.

In *Fear of Falling: The Inner Life of the Middle Class*, Barbara Ehrenreich's follow-up to the 1977 essay on the PMC, Ehrenreich argued that growing PMC class antagonism against working-class people was animated by growing economic fear in reaction to right-wing attacks on social and public services, now combined with countercultural contempt for ordinary people. By the Reagan era, the hippie had morphed into the yuppie, or young urban professional, who could boast of an intense attachment to the nonpareil pleasures and instant gratifications enabled by the American Express card. As economic redistribution from top to bottom came to an end, and rent-seeking capitalists were no longer vilified in the popular imagination, the yuppie briefly took center stage in the American imagination as a figure who pointed the way to a gaudy, self-indulgent future. According to Ehrenreich, the yuppie reconciled 1960s hedonism and 1980s debt-fueled consumerism. Prayer beads became Rolexes, but the tradition-busting ethos was the same: pleasure will set you free. The young urban professional mocked the ideals of economic disinterestedness and elite public service that had characterized the old PMC. The celebration of the pure power of money was embodied both by the fictional Patrick Bateman, the homeless and prostitute-murdering, coke-addled Wall Street trader of *American Psycho*, and the real-life Donald Trump. In *American Psycho*, Bret Easton Ellis makes yuppie sadism seem *transgressively* antiliberal, exciting, and glamorous.

By the 1980s, PMC elite fantasies about ordinary middle-, lower-middle-, and working-class Americans were colored by both yuppie and hippie fantasies: ordinary people were trapped in stultifying stable jobs, deferred gratification, and social conformity. They were like Flaubert's village idiots, but infuriatingly, they enjoyed good pensions and benefits. If the hippies hated the stability achieved by the union-negotiated peace with postwar corporations, yuppies actually went ahead and destroyed the institutions of lifetime-guaranteed employment through leveraged buyouts that led to blue-and then white-collar downsizing. Yuppies were not American psychos or charismatic sociopaths—they were boring, anxious, and conformist— but they did represent a new face of the PMC elite: they served new masters and enjoyed the rewards of that service. When Jack Welch took over General Electric in 1981, he personified as a super yuppie the ethos of management for stockholder value. Welch relied on a cadre of PMC cost cutters and "set out to raise the stock price by cutting the workforce." More than seventy thousand GE employees lost their jobs on Welch's watch, and his managerial abilities were loudly celebrated in the business press and across business schools all over the world. Stockbrokers and upper management were well rewarded for their work in downsizing workforces. Yuppies helped to birth a new world for capitalism, a world of public austerity and private luxury, globalized economies and shiny cities surrounded by devastated hinterlands, a world of offshored labor and lightning-quick capital flows. They executed neoliberalism's orders, and they snorted coke while they were at it, their alleged vanguardism only limited by their credit card limits.

The more Reagan tore away at the social safety net, the more the poor appeared to the fragile middle class as nightmarish doubles of who they would be if they were to lose their toeholds on bourgeois respectability. The PMC saw the classes below them through the eyes of the ruling class, and they could not distance themselves fast enough from the immiserated poor. As downward social mobility became a terrifying reality, poor people were increasingly seen as the monstrous other. Poverty was racialized and the poor were demonized in right-wing talking points. In the time of Reagan, a new narrative of poverty emerged: poor people had no impulse control. They did not live within their means: the story began in the 1960s, when Daniel Moynihan argued that poverty was a question of "culture". By the 1980s, the American middle class was terrified of falling into the classes below it, and its own financial well-being was, objectively speaking, increasingly at risk. In a new age of instability and middle-class fragility, it was hypnotized by the spectacle of the yuppies as a class above and terrified of the classes below.

The framing of such economic strife obscured its material conditions by overemphasizing culture over political economy. Fredric Jameson and other Marxists identified a "cultural turn" in our understanding of social antagonism, eclipsing economic conditions for apparatuses of divining tastes and affects. By the 1990s, the cultural rebels who had gotten PhDs in the 1970s stormed the university and secured tenured positions. They did not pay attention to budgets and administration as much as they were obsessed with their own commitments to cultural transgression, some of which involved wearing jeans to class, smoking pot, sleeping with students, and listening to John Cale, but also enjoying Madonna's MTV videos. Jean Baudrillard had taught us that everything was simulacral, and it did seem as if style had become the most important part of substance, and words become signifiers were permanently untethered from their referents. In the evolution of PMC, antagonism against mainstream culture and ordinary people were mixed up with its smug sense of subcultural superiority.

"Transgressing" the Boundaries of Professionalism

IN 1996, when *Social Text* accepted and published Alan Sokal's "Transgressing the Boundaries: Towards a Transformative Hermeneutics of Quantum Gravity," the editors believed they were publishing the work of what we would call today a "woke" physicist and mathematician. With footnotes citing theorists from Derrida to Guattari and Deleuze, Sokal made the hair-raising claim that

> deep conceptual shifts within twentieth-century science have undermined ... Cartesian-Newtonian metaphysics; revisionist studies in the history and philosophy of science have cast further doubt on its credibility; and, most recently, feminist and poststructuralist critiques have demystified the substantive content of mainstream Western scientific practice, revealing the ideology of domination concealed behind the fa.ade of "objectivity." It has thus become increasingly apparent that physical "reality," no less than social "reality," is at bottom a social and linguistic construct.

In the name of poststructural theory and the radical relativism that masked its liberal pluralism, Sokal's article denied the very foundations of modern science—that we live in a world governed by the laws of physics, which can be observed and described. Eager to support theory-friendly, anti-Enlightenment writing that allowed for the confusion of relativism with relativity, *Social Text* editors Stanley Abramowitz, Bruce Robbins, Andrew Ross and the article's peer reviewers were ready to believe that mathematics and allopathic medicine were just waiting to be disrupted and transgressed by "theory" itself. Sokal's essay on quantum physics seemed to usher in a new matriarchal multiverse governed by unstable but transgressive subatomic particles, zigzagging through reality, ready to blow our minds and bend our genders and our taste cultures.

After Sokal revealed that his article was a hoax designed to reveal the lack of intellectual and scientific standards of judgment in the top journal of cultural studies, the editors responded with condescension, outrage, and defensiveness. Sokal claimed that theory of the poststructuralist kind was a fraud, not based on academic research or evidence, and dependent on ambitious authors making the right noises about bogus bogeymen like science and objectivity. In turn, the editors of *Social Text* claimed that when they first received Sokal's submission, they thought he was a naive science guy who was worthy of encouragement, trying to master theory a bit clumsily and overzealously. After first condescending to him (by allegedly encouraging him), they demonized him when they discovered his article was a hoax. They accused Sokal of unethical behavior and bad faith. The fact was, it was the editors' mistake to have published the article. Its publication did serious damage to the reputation of the humanities, at least within the academy. Physicists and mathematicians and young scientists working in quantum physics and quantum chemistry still study the Sokal affair. Theorists and humanists tend to try to forget it. In any case, there were no professional consequences for any of the editors of the journal. In fact, the reputations of Ross, Aronowitz, and Robbins were burnished in theory circles because they claimed to be fighting the good fight against the reactionary enemies of theory and identity politics. The three editors represented what would become the dominant, PMC-approved identitarian positions in academic circles. It should be noted that the Sokal affair took place during the height of the culture wars in the American academy, and theoretical and cultural studies innovators painted all opponents of their epistemological innovations as reactionaries, trying to hold on to outdated ideas like objectivity and, worse yet, universalism.

The poststructuralist cultural studies theorists despised the oppressive post–World War II liberal consensus as much as the most visionary of neoliberal economists like Alan Greenspan and his overlord, Ayn Rand. That liberal consensus was based on state and corporate support for lifetime employment, labor power, and strong social services and redistributive economic policies. The New Left/cultural studies types hated the liberal consensus as much as the neoliberals. If you do not believe me, do a search for liberal consensus in digitized copies of cultural studies books of the 1990s and you will see it appears only to be dismissed with the patriarchy and heteronormativity and a vaguely Foucauldian idea of "domination." The economic system and the social safety net built by that much despised consensus were already fragilized in the 1990s by years of corporate depredations. As Elizabeth Warren and Teresa Sullivan showed in their 2001 book *The Fragile Middle Class: Americans in Debt,* wage compression and the rising cost of living had forced the American middle class to carry debt to maintain standards of living once achieved through wage growth. Warren and Sullivan showed that middle-class people were unable to live on their salaries and that they were being exploited by financial instruments like credit cards and second mortgages to supplement stagnant wages. They were not going on vacations by borrowing money— they were paying medical bills, college tuition, and the costs of starting their own small businesses after being laid off or having family members laid off from stable jobs. The trends that Warren and Sullivan identified only intensified after their book was published. Economic growth had left most Americans behind, but real estate values continued to rise, despite stock market volatility in the 1990s and early 2000s. Banks discovered that middle- and working-class mortgage debt was an untapped source of profit for creditors as long as housing prices kept going up. Still suffering from wage compression, Americans used their homes for second mortgages to pay for their exploding cost of living. Banks were so eager to refinance debt and offer barely employed people credit during the early aughts: only the flimsiest forms of documentation were needed for homeowners and home buyers to get big loans. These loans would be at the heart of the subprime mortgage meltdown. People were encouraged to buy expensive new homes or refinance their paid-off homes, borrowing money at low interest rates that would balloon in a few years. The banks packaged these almost fraudulent loans, known as subprime mortgages, into complex instruments that marbled good debt and risky debt into things called collateralized debt obligations.

The house of cards came tumbling down when stressed homeowners began to default on their loans. Bear Stearns, an investment bank overexposed to high-risk debt instruments, ran out of money in March 2008. Lehman Brothers went bankrupt that fall, and the stock market and the housing market crashed one after the other. Wealthy people blamed poor people for trying to cash in on a crazy market—but we know that moral failings or a "culture" of indebtedness was not the real cause of the crash. I heard wealthy Americans in my family complain that the crisis was caused by poor people buying flat-screen televisions. Once again, as they did in the Gilded Age, the wealthy found ways of feeling superior to the poor, but this time in the mode of their more virtuous handling of their wealth. Ordinary Americans, it turned out, were ensnared by a sticky web of corruption, financialization, compressed wages, fear of falling, and lack of regulation. For journalists and financial historians like John Cassidy and Adam Tooze, the crash and the ensuing bailout are directly related to the fall of centrist governments around the world.

On September 10, 2008, Hank Paulson, George W. Bush's Treasury secretary, and Ben Bernanke, chairman of the Federal Reserve, went to Congress to urge lawmakers to bail out the collapsing banking sector. In 2009, under the new Obama administration, Timothy Geithner engineered TARP, or the Troubled Asset Relief Program, giving banks $700 million of public money to balance their books. According to Tooze's analysis, the Federal Reserve transferred an additional $5 trillion to non-American banks to guarantee global financial liquidity. In the meantime, between 2007 and 2016, 7.8 million Americans lost their homes to foreclosure. The economic crisis and subsequent bailout exacerbated inequality by every metric and did not lead to significant reform of the financial sector. Bailed-out banks continued to foreclose on the homes of working-class families while refusing to make new loans to creditworthy borrowers. Under an Ivy League–educated African American president, African American family wealth had collapsed. In fact, it is common knowledge that African American and Latino homeowners were hit hardest by the 2008 financial crisis: by 2018, an African American family owned $5.00 in assets for every $100.00 owned by white families. Obama's identity politics did not translate into economic policies that benefited minorities and working-class people.

In the wake of the 2008 crash, and in the midst of Occupy Wall Street–generated protest excitement, John and Barbara Ehrenreich returned to their 1977 critique and declared the "death of a yuppie dream." Their obituary for the yuppie was premature and overly optimistic, but they were writing at a moment when it seemed that the PMC could reinvent itself in solidarity with the working class. The Ehrenreichs, like Christopher Lasch before them, emphasized that the PMC was having difficulty reproducing itself because it had undermined working conditions for all Americans while raising too high the barrier of entry into the credentialed classes. PMC families and their children were reeling from the punishing cost of higher education as well as the narrowing gates of a corrupt meritocracy. In pinning their hopes on the Occupy Wall Street movement, the Ehrenreichs wanted to will the PMC to real political oppositionality. It is undeniable that young, downwardly mobile, college-educated "occupiers" attracted national attention when protestors took over Zucotti Park on Wall Street on September 17, 2011. They were evicted two months later, but the movement articulated a durable formula for describing economic inequality: "we are the 99 percent" set up the antagonism between the 1 percent, or richest segment of the population, and the rest of us, even the top 9 percent, or those members of the PMC. A survey done by City University of New York researchers Ruth Milkman, Stephanie Luce, and Penny Lewis on May 1, 2012, during a massive protest attended by many former occupiers showed that the activists and former occupiers were mostly college-educated, white-collar professionals, majority male, with only 8 percent of occupiers/respondents reporting themselves as blue collar. In their analysis of Occupy, Milkman, Luce, and Lewis emphasized the experience of the core activists, their allegiance to the Canadian anticonsumerist magazine Adbusters, and the inspiration they took from the Arab Spring protests.

One occupier quoted by Milkman, Luce, and Lewis said that "OWS [Occupy Wall Street] was a floating signifier that everybody saw different things in." The idea of the floating signifier was one of the most important tenets of poststructuralist theory. It was based on the linguistic theory of Ferdinand de Saussure applied by Claude Levi-Strauss to the cultural sphere in general. For Saussure, the linguistic signifier was untethered from any referential determination to objects in the empirical world. Saussure's structuralist theory of meaning generated by difference rather than intention was highly influential in the fields of anthropology and literary theory. For Saussure, the combination of the signified (referent) and the signifier (the linguistic unit of meaning) together made up the "sign." Poststructuralism took the principles of linguistics and transferred them to philosophy, culture, and literary texts. Meaning could "float" above the signified world: signifiers became both empty and playful, detached from signifieds or referents. Puns became a form of thinking while "difference" replaced contradiction (in either Hegelian or Marxist terms) as the sinews that held together and determined flexible structures of interpretation. In 1994, Alan Sokal tried to puncture the poststructuralist approach to politics and culture by showing that it was foolish to "apply" poststructural ideas to physics and scientific attempts to describe physical reality, but in 2012, students of theory were happily applying the findings of Saussurean linguistics to one of the most significant popular protest movements of the new millennium. Sokal's project failed to put any of the poststructural nostra to rest, as a generation of theory-trained young people took to the public spaces of New York City to protest a financial system that was in fact very compatible with floating signifiers, radical pluralism, and the untethering of financial values from empirical realities. Signs emptied of meaning gave stock brokers, financial analysts, and occupiers alike a sophisticated way of talking about value, cons, lies, and grifts.

In the same set of interviews, activist Arun Gupta talks about Ernesto Laclau and Chantal Mouffe's concept of chains of equivalence, where everyone's grievances could be seen as equal to everyone else's grievances. Laclau and Mouffe's tortured theory of populism risked no popular appeal, but it created the illusion of analyzing a "new" form of politics. The highly educated members of Occupy fetishized the procedural regulation and management of discussion to reach consensus about all collective decisions. Daily meetings or General Assemblies were managed according to a technique called the progressive stack. Its fanatical commitment to proceduralism an administrative strategy suppressed real discussion of priorities or politics and ended up promoting only the integrity of the progressive stack itself. Protecting the stack became more important than formulating political demands that might have resonated with hundreds of millions of Americans whose lives were being directly destroyed by finance capital. PMC/New Left ideas about mass movements dominated Occupy's dreams of politics and limited the effectiveness of its activism. Demographically and politically, Occupy was squarely a PMC elite formation: "Changing the Subject" is a fundamentally sympathetic account of Occupy's politics, but its demographic findings about the movement paint a stark portrait of the typical occupier, who was downwardly mobile, male, young, white, educated at an elite university, and in student loan and credit card debt. The heavy union representation at Occupy reflected the predominance of unionized graduate students.

By 2016, PMC elites became even more worshipful of money and more contemptuous of ordinary people: Hillary Clinton as a successor to Barack Obama was the incarnation of PMC values and the Democratic Party's power elite. Under Hillary Clinton, the Democratic Party would no longer concern itself with working-class interests, the ones her husband had ignored despite his good old boy style: the exercise of power would consist of protecting capitalism while setting up a carefully groomed lineup of diverse, donor-friendly candidates to run for the highest offices in the land. Wall Street and Silicon Valley donors would be appeased. No one to her left dared to challenge her run, except for Bernie Sanders, senator from Vermont. Clinton was the PMC elite's dream candidate, a sign that the class had completely taken over the once unruly Democratic Party that had formerly represented working-class interests. Clinton was an alleged shoo-in, the most qualified presidential candidate ever, a woman who loved Wall Street and the ruling class, a Lean-in pseudo-feminist who wanted to inspire girls to become *girl bosses*. Clinton's defeat was not just a blow to centrist rule; it was an angry rejection of the hypocrisy of the PMC *tout court*. Because of the rise of right-wing populism, political commentators were forced to deal with the election in terms of class formation, which they quickly transformed into geographical and cultural differences that divided America and needed to be understood as such.

From the 1990s, transgressive antiprofessionalism had become the opium of the vanguard corps of PMC elites. Angela Nagle's book *Kill All Normies: On Line Culture Wars from 4Chan and Tumblr to Trump and the Alt-Right* angered these cultural studies transgression worshippers. Like Sokal, Nagle is a proponent of the Old Left, but unlike Sokal, she was not a tenured professor in a STEM field. Nagle has been cancelled by scholars writing the kinds of things that Sokal parodied. Liberal academics could not bear to see their love of subcultural insider knowledge questioned or criticized, especially by an adjunct and junior scholar. Since the publication of Nagle's book, which was critical of her work, Gabriella Coleman, holder of the Wolf Chair in Scientific and Technological Literacy at McGill University, has worked tirelessly to blacklist and deplatform the Irish scholar. Nagle, who worked for years as an adjunct and journalist in the para-academic world, has little institutional power or standing in comparison with Coleman, the prize-winning ethnographer of Anonymous. Nagle suggested that Coleman's 2014 book *Hacker, Hoaxer, Whistleblower, Spy* was one example of the feverish academic embrace of transgression and its antinormie animus. Nagle argues in passing that Coleman lost her distance to her ethnographic subjects of study— Internet provocateurs like /weev/, Andrew Aurenheimer, convicted and sentenced in 2012 of hacking AT&T. Coleman loves transgression, the kind parodied by Sokal, and her book is rife with gushing accounts of her relationships with online microcelebrities. Coleman is unfazed by the fact that /weev/ turned out to be an anti-Semitic, neo-Nazi webmaster of the far right website Daily Stormer. In contrast to Coleman, Nagle argued that the Left should be embracing the normative forces of class struggle, not the subcultural transgressions and exploits of people like Aurenheimer. Nagle believes in mass, working-class-based coalitions and movements, not subcultural fetish politics, which she finds undermines the forms of solidarity that are needed for the long struggles of the future. Parody, civil dissent, reasoned debate, contradiction, and polemics are useless, however, against people who see the world as a series of opportunities for transgressing boundaries and celebrating floating signifiers and Deleuzian lines of flight.

In fact, Sokal's and Nagel's object of critique—the academic fetish for the transgression of "norms"—has become a "progressive" PMC elite strategy for gaining media attention. With the help of private foundations that are tireless in promoting their antiworker, antiacademic freedom agenda, today's academic entrepreneurs are using social causes to further their own agendas. Academic research, at least in the humanities and social sciences, is being subtly shaped by the agendas of the ruling class— sometimes directly by mega-wealthy individuals, but also by private foundations endowed by mega-wealthy individuals, and their liberal-minded employees in para-academic positions in the media. It's not even clear that these professionals and opportunists understand the part they're playing in undermining academic freedom or professional autonomy.

Take, for example, the role a once obscure private foundation, the Pulitzer Center, played in catapulting the 1619 Project into the center of the national debate about race, slavery, and the teaching and framing of American history. The Pulitzer Center allegedly "raises awareness of underreported global issues through direct support of quality journalism across all media platforms and a unique program of education and public outreach." The Pulitzer Center's most prolific donor is Emily Rauh Pulitzer and the Emily Rauh Pulitzer Foundation. Widow of newspaperman Joseph Pulitzer, Rauh Pulitzer is also a major donor to the arts.

In 2019, the Pulitzer Center collaborated with the *New York Times Magazine* to launch the 1619 Project, directed by journalist Nikole Hannah-Jones. The Project was launched to commemorate the four-hundredth anniversary of the arrival of the first enslaved peoples in the American colonies—for its collaborators, the real birthday of the United States of America. Included as part of the *New York Times Magazine* in August 2019, the 1619 Project caused quite a media sensation: copies of the Sunday *Times* in which it was included quickly sold out. The Project rewrites the American revolution as a revolt of slaveholders against the British abolitionists and, in its first iteration, argues that the United States of America should be understood as first and foremost a country founded in defense of the institution of slavery. Against the historical evidence that the British monarchy was not taking anti–Atlantic slave trade positions before 1776 and that the colonists themselves were divided on the issue, Hannah-Jones leads a group of writers, scholars, and journalists to dismiss the work of historians of colonial America in order to promote their view of the nation as hopelessly and exceptionally racist.

Just as the editors of *Social Text* and their colleagues were happy to transgress the norms of the scientific and mathematical communities two decades ago, the 1619 Project rejects the norms of historical research. In the case of the 1619 Project, however, the *New York Times* is not a small academic journal: the fear of offending the powerful forces, funders and donors who support the Project through private foundations, has cast a pall over the debate around its findings. The authors of the Project reject all criticism of it: they believe that their findings do not depend on the research consensus and archival evidence sorted through by a scholarly community of historians. Using her new clout and massive audience, Nikole Hannah-Jones led the way in dismissing the accepted scholarship that had been done on colonial America as simply the highly biased work of white males. Lifetimes of careful, empirical research were simply no match for massive foundation dollars backed by one of the largest media companies in the world.

It is clear that powerful financial and media interests are behind the promotion of the 1619 Project and its bold attempt to change the way we understand American history and historical research itself. The Project is on top of everything, a bold attempt to eliminate historical materialism from the teaching and writing of American history while destroying the possibility of solidarity in the American working class. Socialist historians on the pages of the World Socialist Web Site

(WSWS.org) have been some of the Project's most vocal and astute critics, but their work is not supported or funded by a dense and tangled network of foundations and media elites. The Project wants to lay out a subtle but clear lesson for its readers: the impossibility of working-class solidarity. The World Socialist Web Site is also one of the few media outlets to have publicized the fact that under pressure from historians, the *New York Times* and Hannah-Jones have quietly abandoned their initial claims that 1619 was the "true founding moment" of the United States. Rather than publish a retraction or a correction of their claim, they have quietly softened their thesis on the website of the project by claiming that the Project's goal is about centering slavery and the contributions of black Americans in relationship to American identity and narrativized nationhood. No trace of the earlier hyperbolic claims remains on the 1619 Project website, but researchers at WSWS.org retained a copy of the original site's thesis about the founding the United States.

Few stop to ask why such powerful and affluent donors and organizations would be so invested in such a historical project—particularly one that elicited such strong counterarguments from widely respected historians. In its focus on race and the singularity of the history of American slavery, the 1619 Project ignores historical and economic conditions that might make slavery comparable to other forms of exploitation—chattel slavery and serfdom being two premodern examples and the wage slavery of industrial capitalism being another. In doing so, it furthers a cherished liberal rallying cry of our time: that interracial solidarity among the working class is simply impossible—better not even to try to establish a universalist critique of capitalism. The leading thinkers of the 1619 Project insist that it is race, not class, that has created the essential social and economic fault line in America. Racism is, they argue, a transhistorical fact written into our national character.

This view fits in nicely with the story of American pluralism promoted by postwar private foundation–sponsored ideology. From a pluralist point of view, African Americans are a distinctive and powerful interest group who, because of their particular history, should advocate for themselves and for reparations for the singular suffering they endured under the particularly brutal institution of American slavery—there's no need for them to join labor unions with other workers whose experiences can never be a perfect match for their own. Other "groups," Hispanics, Latinos, Asian Americans, Native Americans, and so on, can each advocate separately for their special interests. They just need to come up with competing versions of their historical singularity and find powerful donors who will support them in publicizing their cause.

In the early 1970s, just as the policies of deindustrialization and austerity were being perfected as instruments of class warfare in the United States, Jonathan Cobb and Richard Sennett interviewed the janitor "Ricca Kartides" (a pseudonym) for *The Hidden Injuries of Class*. The young sociologists discovered that Kartides, who worked as a janitor, felt humiliated every day by his job and its low social status. He was, however, on his salary alone, able to buy his own home so that his children wouldn't have to live in the building he cleaned. Kartides's ability to buy a house and support a family on his wages is unimaginable today. Today, the average janitor, who makes $24,000 a year, may be ostensibly or formally equal to the average CEO, who makes $14 million a year, but that equality seems like a cruel joke played by capitalism and liberal democracy on the working class.

The radical and material difference in average income between janitor and CEO should be intolerable to everyone who is not a capitalist, but PMC elites have internalized the values of the meritocracy so deeply that they cannot see the radical nature of this difference in incomes as essentially different from all other kinds of difference. As social and economic stratification intensifies across the globe, it spawns a series of political crises and shocks that have shaken centrist governments that have promoted neoliberal, austerity-driven policies for the past fifty years. It is in the face of such a destabilized polity and an ongoing political and economic crisis that a renewed Left must produce political critique and a cultural program informed by the needs of mass politics. If the Left refuses to produce better, more historically grounded accounts of the past, ones that situate contemporary class and cultural conflict in the context of historical struggles for universal principles of equality, dignity, and emancipation, liberals will not do it for us. Liberals have abandoned history, because they have to believe they are superior to elites of the past and the contemporary working class at the same time. Members of the PMC believe themselves to be virtuous vanguardists, floating above historical forms and conditions, transgressing boundaries and inventing new ways of being and seeing. It is hard to argue with them, because they do not accept debate as a meaningful form of the advancement of knowledge. For them, every conflict is moral, not intellectual or political. Sokal failed to stop the proliferation of Americanized ahistorical poststructuralist lines of research in the humanities. Nagel reframed the notion of transgression, but found herself banished from academia. I have no illusions about the power of my critique against the dominant tendencies in academia today, but I will not stop criticizing opportunistic forms of antihistorical, and antimaterialist, antiprofessional work in my profession.

The PMC Has Children

FROM THE VERY MOMENT OF CONCEPTION, which for PMC parents is always a "choice," the future child and infant possesses "potential" that has to be both optimized and maximized. PMC mothers have to do prenatal yoga while setting up intra-uterine Mozart streams on pregnant bellies. Preparing for a child is just the beginning of a torturous and expensive preoccupation for today's elites. PMC people are both terrified of and thrilled by procreation, because children cannot help but amplify social anxieties about competition. For Paula Fass, fear is one of the distinctive features of contemporary middle-class parenting, as middle-class parents "imagine what an unsuccessful child might face in the future." Even with full-time hired help, PMC working parents are stressed about infant pedagogy and proper stimulation while pulling down the double salaries that allow them to maintain upper-middle-class consumption habits. Babies are notoriously sensual beings, both dependent and hedonistic. Their helplessness and drive for pleasure represent an existential threat to the Puritanism of American elites. It is not surprising, then, that managing the development of children into successful adults dominates the ethos of PMC parenting. For them, the 40 percent of American children conceived outside of marriage and the upper middle class are deemed unworthy of collective attention or public concern. You don't have to be a socialist to see the reproduction of class privilege played out in the most dramatic and extreme ways in childcare, children's health, and children's education.

In her best seller *Perfect Madness: Motherhood in an Age of Anxiety*, Judith Warner decries the anguished, competitive perfectionism of contemporary upper-middle-class motherhood. Since Warner published her book in 2006, the anxiety she describes has only intensified. Megan Erickson argues that these anxieties and fears are not unjustified, "given the increasing stratification even within the top 1% of the country's earners as the 2008–2009 financial crisis has only exacerbated the class war that those on top wage against all those below them." Parenting fads have become hot commodities in America's wealthiest neighborhoods. Perfectionist PMC parents are crusading class formation pioneers: they will not hesitate to humiliate nannies, babysitters, teachers, grandmothers, and other parents about the horrific effects of vaccines, screen time, tickling, dolls with faces, video games, cigarette-shaped candy, or sugar in general. With COVID-19, children of the wealthiest Americans who are enrolled in private schools enjoy full-time private tutors and smaller class sizes on Zoom and/or in person, mitigating risk and maximizing stimulation and education.

Around 1900, the emerging PMC became concerned with children's welfare from a public policy standpoint. As Judith Sealander notes, social reform movements promoted a powerful vision of the role of government in redressing social ills, especially when it came to childcare and maternal health. But as the twentieth century came to an end, PMC elites became fully neoliberalized and joined their voices to the right-wing denunciation of "big government" and its allegedly debilitating "handouts." Bill Clinton's Personal Responsibility and Work Opportunity Act of 1996, or welfare reform, inaugurated a relentless war against the youngest, the poorest, and the most vulnerable people in the country. To qualify for welfare, the poorest American mother had to find a job and keep it, even though she could not afford childcare on her meager salary. Austerity and "personal responsibility" have been the sigils under which benefit-cutting austerity policies were forged to torture those who had the least in an affluent society. In the United States, there is always enough for tax cuts for the rich and never enough money for social programs for children and their caretakers. In matters of child welfare, the PMC elite believe that the social surplus, or surplus value generated by the totality of economic activity, should be enjoyed by the children of the wealthy few, while the majority of working-class and working-poor children and their caretakers are consigned to lives of punishment, surveillance, and parsimonious rewards.

In his enduring best seller *Baby and Child Care*, first published in 1945 as the baby boomers were taking their first baby steps, Benjamin Spock advised anxious postwar parents to trust themselves with their babies. Dr. Spock became one of the most influential experts in child-rearing for post– World War II America. Popularizing psychoanalytic ideas about pleasure and projection, he played a critical role in the formation of new PMC identities. Spock advocated against traditional ideas about infant discipline and told young, newly prosperous blue- and white-collar parents to trust themselves with their babies. Despite the fact that Spock warned parents against faddish child-rearing counsel, his own advice was packaged in a popular book that has been hailed as the American twentieth century's second best seller, after the Bible. Dr. Spock was also an outspoken, anti– Vietnam War, New Left activist. Conservatives blamed him for fomenting countercultural revolt and encouraging young people to be self-indulgent rebels since their Dr. Spock–reading parents had not disciplined them as infants. His advice, however, had a paradoxical tone, familiar to consumers of self-help literature. Dr. Spock reminded his readers relentlessly that they were the ones in the know. "You can read books and articles, but the main way you will learn is to be observant in a meaningful way. That means spending time, looking and listening to your baby, not just feeding and cleaning him . . . and then trusting yourself. Because you do know more than you do."

In the 1970s, as budding PMC boomers dabbled in "Eastern" religions, privileged self-exploration over tradition, and pursued emotional and sexual experimentation, they looked at the working class as out-of-touch authoritarians who married for life and lived in traditional two-parent families. Today, after decades of austerity, working-class families and kinship networks are at a breaking point. Jefferson Cowie and Jennifer Silva have shown that working-class Americans today have more unstable family lives and greater instances of divorce and single parenthood than their PMC counterparts. PMC people are far more likely to marry and remain married. They rarely if ever marry outside their class. The PMC family has become a veritable redoubt from which class privilege is reproduced, but with stingy parental leave policies, increasing health care costs, compressed wages, and the exploding cost of higher education, the PMC family feels beleaguered and threatened by the possibility of failing to raise the most "successful" children. In the time of COVID-19, these anxieties have not gone away. They have been exacerbated.

In 2014, Yale Law School faculty members Amy Chua and Jed Rubenfeld proved Marx right by publishing T*he Triple Package: How Three Unlikely Traits Explain the Rise and Fall of Cultural Groups in America*, a book that was purely determined by the "material life conditions" of its authors. After the runaway success of 2011's *Battle Hymn of the Tiger Mother*, a best-selling parenting memoir about Chua's attempts to optimize her daughters' childhoods and childhood activities, Tina Bennett, Chua's literary agent, no doubt hoped for a follow-up volume that would fly off the shelves like the first book. Chua's best seller was an irritating but highly entertaining read. When the *Wall Street Journal* excerpted a part of Battle Hymn under the title "Why Chinese Mothers Are Superior," the Tiger Mother brand hit pay dirt. Despite her repeated protestations that her book and its title were both self-disparaging and self-reflexive, readers took her memoir as a parenting how-to guide.

Chua and Rubenfeld argued in perfect matrimonial sync that successful "cultural groups" have the triple package: (1) a superiority complex, (2) an inferiority complex, and—wait for it—(3) better impulse control. This last quality, famously (and falsely) lacking in those who happen to be African American, Mexican American, or just poor, explains why groups that do not defer satisfaction fail to "succeed." Chua and Rubenfeld offer repackaged social Darwinist–tinged, culture-of-poverty arguments that are trotted out every few years to justify the entrenched immiseration of large swathes of the American population. Who are successful in America, according to the two Yale law professors, one now disgraced? A narrow band of wealthy meritocrats, of course. In Chua and Rubenfeld's United States, there is no polity, no class, no society, no collective endeavor, no social responsibility: there are only "cultural groups" vying for advantages in the fields of prestige and business. Their idea of a better world? The abolition of the whole idea of a "group." America will be a better place when there are only successful and unsuccessful individuals, all competing on an allegedly even playing field.

Despite Rubenfeld's apparent professional "success," he has proven himself woefully lacking in impulse control. In August 2020, Rubenfeld was quietly suspended from Yale Law School for sexual misconduct, including predatory and harassing behavior toward female students. Recently, Yale Law School students have demanded his permanent removal. A group of students is petitioning the president of Yale, Peter Salovey, to have Rubenfeld permanently removed from the faculty.

As the gulf between rich and poor has widened, while social mobility has decreased in every racial and ethnic group, the PMC home has become a laboratory of increasingly lavish and expensive childcare equipment and demanding child-rearing techniques that now include outright bribes and elaborate cheating strategies to help their children succeed at any cost. The Varsity Blues case, which revealed that rich and super-rich parents were paying college counselor Rick Singer hundreds of thousands of dollars to get their children through the "side door" of athletic admission into college, is only the logical outcome of ruling-class determination to guarantee their children's "success."

The class war from above has had dire consequences for all American children and their caretakers, but the toll it has taken on the poorest families is staggering. Recently, the Urban Institute found that children are the poorest segment of American society, with 22 percent of American children living in poverty, while 38.8 percent of American children have experienced some form of poverty in their lives. The numbers for African American children are even more grim, with 38.8 percent of African American children living in poverty and 75.4 percent of African children having lived in poverty.

While PMC parenting books promote the extraordinary measures to which elite parents will go to guarantee their children's "success," D. W. Winnicott praised *ordinary* devoted mothers for bonding with their infants in a way that gave an astonishing majority of human beings the mental health to be able to enjoy play, creativity, and richness of experience. Winnicott had an expansive, gender-neutral idea of the caretaker; however, for the sake of brevity, I use his term the "good enough mother" in discussing his ideas. In learning to take care of an infant, the "good enough mother" loves her baby but responds imperfectly to its needs; a good enough, but not perfect, caretaker begins to adapt to her baby's growing physical and emotional capacity to endure frustration by sometimes failing to respond immediately to the baby's demands. These necessary failures reflect the mother's absorption in other tasks and represent opportunities for the baby to establish a healthy tolerance for frustration as well as an incipient recognition of self and other.

In his introduction to *The Child, the Family and the Outside World*, published in 1964, Winnicott writes,

> I am trying to draw attention to the immense contribution to the individual and the society which the ordinary good mother with

> her husband in support makes at the beginning, and which she does simply through being devoted to her infant. Is not this contribution of the devoted mother unrecognized precisely because it is immense? If this contribution is accepted it follows that everyone who is sane, everyone feels himself to be a person in the world, and for whom the world means something, every happy person, is in infinite debt to a woman.... The result of such recognition of the maternal role ... will not be gratitude or even praise. The result will be a lessening in ourselves of a fear. If our society delays making full acknowledgment of this dependence which is a historical fact in the initial stage of development in every individual, there must remain a block to ease and complete health, a block that comes from a fear.

It is clear from this passage that Winnicott believes that the care of infants is a social and public good to which each caretaker contributes in an infant's earliest days. Caretakers cannot be parsimonious in their gifts of love and sacrifice of sleep and libido to the dependent infant: their generosity provides the child with an inalienable legacy of security and fearlessness when facing the challenges of growing up in an uncertain world. The stressed and deprived caretaker who demands repayment or calculates the debt of a child is one who instills fear and anxiety, a state that our present-day world, made by fiscal austerity and economic sadism, knows only too well.

Although it is difficult to imagine a time when the richness of childhood experience was embraced as a public good, it was only sixty years ago that Winnicott built his psychoanalytic theories on the idea of collective and mutual responsibility for dependents and their caretakers. Winnicott's 1964 optimism about overcoming fearfulness should be both inspiring and worrying for us today when fear of falling and fear of failing seem to be generalized conditions. In postwar Great Britain, Winnicott welcomed the redistribution of social surplus that would allow the greatest number of Britons to experience the richness and health of his own privileged childhood. He admits openly that his happy childhood allowed him to expand upon his ability for observation, empathy, and play. These qualities and abilities are part of a human legacy that every baby on the planet deserves to enjoy. Winnicott always argued that the support of a baby's caretaker is a social and collective responsibility. The unglamorous infrastructural support of good enough parenting is the good enough state, a social democratic system of redistributive support for those people who take care of the neediest and most helpless human beings. If the good enough mother can be cherished as a cultural and collective inheritance and social good, we can begin to build a society where dependency is not feared or demonized. We can begin to build a world where happy parents and stable childhoods are a collective good and no child will ever be "fine-tuned" to "succeed."

The PMC Reads a Book

ON JANUARY 16, 2017, to ready its readers for the shock of the Trump inauguration, the *New York Times* published Michiko Kakutani's portrait of Barack Obama. The "reader-in-chief," Obama was the sainted apotheosis of the PMC elite. He did not enjoy inherited wealth; he was a man of the people, found and promoted by the meritocracy. He was liberalism's dream come true. If we believed in him, then we could believe that social mobility was a "solution" to racism and inequality.

When Obama's heir apparent, Hillary Clinton, lost the 2016 election to Donald Trump, *Times* readers needed solace. The *Times* delivered. "Not since Lincoln has there been a president as fundamentally shaped in his life, convictions and outlook on the world by reading and writing as Barack Obama." In Obama's own words, reading allowed him to "slow down" and put himself in "someone else's shoes." Obama was paraphrasing Atticus Finch, hero of *To Kill a Mockingbird*. In Harper Lee's award-winning novel about a lynching in Maycomb, Alabama, that took place during the Depression, Atticus teaches his daughter Jean Louise/Scout and readers a critical lesson about literature and empathy: "You never understand a person until you consider things from his point of view . . . until you climb into his skin and walk around in it." For Obama, as for most liberal readers, that metaphorical walk takes place through the act of reading. At the end of the Obama presidency, we were bombarded with studies about how reading literature expanded our capacity for understanding the experiences of others. Atticus and Obama showed us that individual acts of empathy and private self-cultivation would produce justice and understanding in a world torn apart by racism and violence. For liberals, this narrative was reassuring: Atticus was not just genteel and antiracist but he was the most virtuous member of his community and a member of the PMC. As a country lawyer, Atticus also became the ethical center of a barbaric and racist world.

In 2010, on the fiftieth anniversary of the novel's publication, NPR celebrated Harper Lee's fiction with a frothy article in praise of the book: one of the interviewees made sure to emphasize that Oprah Winfrey called *To Kill a Mockingbird* "our national novel." In the 1970s, *To Kill a Mockingbird* was an embarrassing curiosity of Cold War propaganda, but in the Obama administration's Common Core curriculum for ninth-grade language arts, *To Kill a Mockingbird* once again occupied pride of place in the canon and tradition of post–World War II American literature. The Obama administration wanted to revive the early 1960s era of high liberalism, but in style only. Although Obama had the opportunity, especially in his first term, to invest new federal funds into public education, his administration was reluctant to match the mobilization that took place in 1959, when the USSR's launch of Sputnik forced Americans to match Soviet investment in both science (STEM) research and the humanities. Obama's Common Core curriculum was allegedly a smarter set of federal standards imposed by a well-educated president to reform the dumbed-down, standardized test–oriented federal education reform instituted by his predecessor, George W. Bush, in the form of No Child Left Behind. Obama's educational reforms, however, did not spur a massive reinvestment in public schools and public universities.

As both Diane Ravitch and Megan Kilpatrick have argued, educational reform is a euphemism for an ongoing war against unionized workers and the lower ranks of white-collar professionals. Fomenting public panic about the state of American schools, educational reformers, supported by for-profit corporations and not-for-profit private foundations, set out to create new assessment regimes to reward and punish teachers with merit pay and austerity budgets. For the past four decades, politicians have been trotting out the "schools are failing our children" as high neoliberal strategy in their antiworker rhetoric, attacking unionized public school teachers by undermining job security and their creative and intellectual autonomy in their classrooms. Improvement of educational outcomes for students is directly related to teacher compensation, smaller class sizes, and adequate funding, but under the Clinton, G. Bush, G. W. Bush, and Obama administrations, education reform has been designed to punish teachers for poor student performance. It is no accident that school teachers' union strikes from Chicago to West Virginia were the first signs that workers were not going to put up with austerity policies any longer. In recent years, teachers' strikes and their organized advocacy for their communities and their students provided some small signs of hope in labor action during times of ideological chaos. Let's not forget that in the 1980s, Bill Clinton made national waves by courageously "standing up" to teachers' unions, which became a part of the centrist politicians' playbook to curry favor with conservtives. As governor of Arkansas, Clinton listened to think tank elites and proposed raising educational standards without raising school budgets. To improve Arkansas's educational attainment ranking at forty-eighth out of fifty states, Clinton imposed a standards test on teachers. In return for passing the required teacher testing as law, Clinton pushed through a slight tax increase. The Heritage Foundation had found that Arkansas citizens' lawsuits to maintain per-student funding levels at $5,400 was a sign of public profligacy that needed to be tamed. Bill Clinton agreed. Inciting moral panic about the state of public education has been a political expedient for liberals and conservatives alike. Bill Clinton's unique style was able to combine post-1968 institutionalized identity politics with a fervor for austerity and budget cutting that made the wealthiest Democratic Party donors as happy as their Republican counterparts.

In 2011, *Harvard Business Review* called for federal curriculum reform that would encourage creativity, complexity, curiosity, and collaboration. Shortly thereafter, then president Obama hired Yale literature major David Coleman, an assessment "expert" with an "interest" in underserved populations, to oversee the reinvigoration of the language arts requirements in the Common Core. Obama and Coleman were interested, like all educational reformers, in "raising standards." Their way of doing it? Through a program branded Race to the Top (RTT), which included the usual assessment (testing) of students and concomitant budgetary rewards and punishments for schools and teachers. Whatever the effectiveness of Common Core and RTT in raising educational attainment standards, the Obama administration left 19.3 percent of American children under the age of five living in extreme poverty. Coleman left his government position to become grand master of the meritocracy, or CEO of the College Board, the highly profitable "nonprofit" organization that oversees the SATs, GREs, and MCATs and all the multiple-choice exams that are meant to predict future academic success of test takers by sorting them into ordinary and extraordinary students.

Coleman, like every other Obama appointee, brought a brilliant pedigree to the administration. Like every literature and English major at Yale (including the author of this book and past and future National Security Agency/Central Intelligence Agency agents, such as super-spy James Jesus Angleton), Coleman was indoctrinated with the idea that close reading is the highest form of human intellectual activity. The Yale literature departments produced and promoted the Cold War based, New Criticism fetish of untangling complex texts: its fundamental methodology relied on the denial of context, whether social, historical, or political. Only under the myopic scrutiny of a good, close reading would an obdurate, clam-like text give up its iridescent pearl of gorgeous meaning. Yale and New Critics hated vulgarity and simplification in any form. Under Coleman, Common Core was shaped by the demands of close reading. When Common Core instituted a new federal test for language arts, the formidable DBQ, document-based questions, bore all the hallmarks of Yale-brewed "close readings." The problem was that DBQ were not questions at all. In the case of *To Kill a Mockingbird*, students were expected to provide document-based evidence for a carefully pre-prepared thesis. (My son was told to show how the novel argues for the importance of "taking a stand.")

So the answer would be that Atticus Finch appears as the one person in Maycomb capable of standing up to racists and rabid dogs: he is the bringer of a civilizing violence meant to protect and seal the community of the righteous. Lee's novel is filled with hatred of the angry, defiant, pleasure-seeking poor white people represented by the awful Ewells. Burris Ewell, the youngest son of that accursed family, arrives at school covered in lice. Burris's sister Mayella also has serious personal hygiene issues and is sexually needy and dishonest; the father of this accursed clan, Bob Ewell, cannot control his impulses for sex, revenge, or violence. Not surprisingly, the Ewells also live on public assistance. Bob assaults his daughter and frames African American Tom Robinson for the crime. Mayella perjures herself in court and accuses Robinson, a man she desired, of the violence inflicted upon her by her father. Atticus successfully defends Robinson in court, but Robinson is convicted despite the exculpating evidence. After his conviction, a mob lynches him while he tries to escape imprisonment. At the end of the novel, Bob Ewell is still angry about Finch's defense of the innocent man, so he tries to kill the two younger Finches. During his attempt at double homicide, he is conveniently murdered by town shut-in Boo Radley.

In the opening scene of the novel, the Cunninghams, poor, noble farmers and foils to the yucky Ewells, pay Atticus's legal fees in hickory nuts. When Scout asks Atticus if the Finches are poor, Atticus tells Scout that the Finches are poor, but not as poor as the Cunninghams. Atticus explains to Scout that the "proud" Cunninghams, whose farm is mortgaged to the hilt, will not take public assistance. The Cunninghams are virtuous poor people. The Ewells are bad poor people: they take public help. With more than half of American children having experienced public assistance at some point or another in their short lives, it seems sadistic to make them read a novel about a noble, virtuous lawyer and the evil public assistance–abusing poor people trying to kill his family. If poor ninth graders pay attention in their language arts classes, they must feel humiliated by their family's willingness to take what the worthy poor of Harper Lee's novel refuse.

It is clear that the ideological message of *To Kill a Mockingbird* underwrote Bill Clinton's 1996 welfare reform. Just as Clinton attacked teachers when he was governor of Arkansas, he attacked welfare and welfare recipients as president. In creating more punishing systems of social support, Clinton, like Harper Lee, promoted the idea that welfare creates dependency and corruption in the poor. Like Lee, he promoted the idea of the deserving poor and the undeserving poor. When Bill Clinton transformed welfare into TANF, or Temporary Assistance for Needy Families, his policy makers turned poor children into the "good" deserving poor and their parents into lazy shirkers who deserved punishment and austerity. Neoliberal policies argue that social safety nets do not catch people falling down; they trap people from rising up. For Lee's novelistic support of such views of the poor, she received a Pulitzer Prize, a National Medal of Freedom (from President George W. Bush), and a National Medal of Arts (from President Barack Obama).

The novel predicted the triumphs of the post-1968 PMC: the moral rectitude of the virtuous lawyer and his high-spirited daughter renders the solution to racism attractive to the establishment—work on individual capacities for empathy and walking in another human being's shoes; read books; have righteous feelings. *To Kill a Mockingbird* was an extraordinarily effective piece of Cold War anti-Communist propaganda: based on a liberal fantasy that antiracism is about good white people defending helpless black people against bad (poor) white people, it created an image of American liberalism that was a powerful tool for winning hearts and minds at home and around the world.

In July 2015, HarperCollins published *Go Set a Watchman*, a sequel to *To Kill a Mockingbird*. Reviewers were disappointed with *Watchman*, not only in the quality of its writing but also because it revealed that Atticus was a member of the Ku Klux Klan. In the novel, he confesses his affiliation to the grown-up Scout, who now lives in New York City and is home in Alabama on vacation. Although the *New York Times* and Kakutani worried about the bitter disappointment that Lee's fans would experience after discovering that Atticus Finch was a racist, the second novel is proof that Lee was actually an ambivalent propagandist. Historical accounts and archival evidence have long confirmed that Klan membership and lynch mobs were made up of educated, wealthy white people who were upstanding citizens of their communities. Many of them, like Atticus, were educated professionals.

If Lee was trying to correct the false, elitist image of racism promoted by *To Kill a Mockingbird*, Kakutani is oblivious to the writer's attempt at historical self-correction. In fact, Kakutani's 2016 portrait of Obama the reader and the thoughtful man is pure ideology. Obama's bookish empathy had distinct limitations. He deported more undocumented immigrants than any other president before him. The post-2008 bank bailout saved bankers but threw millions of Americans out of their homes as they defaulted on usurious mortgages. Obama governed for Wall Street interests, his hand guided by PMC elites, and not for the working classes and those who were victims of banking chicanery and malfeasance. Was it possible that Obama empathized more with Jamie Dimon, CEO of JP Morgan Chase, than with ordinary African American families who lost their homes and livelihoods because of the financial crisis?

In a country that imagined itself uniquely capable of leveling all playing fields and creating equality of opportunity for an astounding array of people of all genders, races, sexualities, gender identifications, and so on, American institutions are increasingly adept at distributing rewards for intelligence and hard work to the few—the suffering and exclusion of the many be damned. In fact, since the 1970s, PMC elites have come to enjoy astounding levels of economic and psychic stability, something to which working-class, non-college-educated people can lay only the feeblest of claims. Furthermore, as Ann Case and Angus Deaton show, a dramatic decline in life expectancy and well-being among middle-aged, non-Hispanic working-class whites without high school degrees has taken on the characteristics of a massive public health epidemic. Unfortunately, *deaths of despair* is a term with which we have all become much too familiar. Unsurprisingly, COVID-19 has proved itself much more lethal in working-class communities of color: PMC workers who can stay home to do their work can enjoy an added health advantage in the age of the pandemic.

At the beginning of the eighteenth century, when the labor of others allowed for European bourgeois elites to use their leisure time to cultivate sensibility and sensitivity in an allegedly disinterested manner, a select group of men and women of leisure came to imagine new forms of sociability and intersubjectivity. Today's capitalists and PMC elites are also into self-cultivation, but their anxiety about their "privilege" makes them work very hard to humiliate others and project themselves tirelessly as a cultural and political vanguard, doing things to themselves of which ordinary people are incapable. PMC elites are always experimenting with themselves: from returning to the "land" under the aegis of new communalism to keto diets, only drinking sewage-laden raw water, and intermittent fasting, their self-indulgence is always a kind of sanctimonious austerity. In terms of etiquette and new forms of mutual address, PMC elites have pioneered a language of liberal tolerance that the working classes have not mastered. PMC elites, consciously or unconsciously, want to humiliate their adversaries by attributing to them a desperate lack of intelligence, empathy, and virtue.

When Kakutani interviewed Obama and he paraphrased Atticus Finch on how not to be a racist, the PMC elite was deifying a mode of reading that was meant to build a set of weak but socially legible links between people in closed-off, insular worlds of sensibilities and sensitivities. Obama, Kakutani, and the early Harper Lee play important roles in inculcating us with the values of American pluralism, here seen as a top-down lesson in the incorporation of professionalized, liberal protocols of self-improvement. Other people, other experiences, only exist to the extent that they can expand our capacity for empathy and feeling. Obama and Kakutani were teaching us all a lesson about how to deal with our cultural inheritance: their PMC didacticism offers lessons we should refuse to learn. Let us read Atticus Finch as a political project and the novel in which he exists as a piece of well-crafted, anti–welfare state, antisocialist propaganda. Reading matters deeply, but not in the way Obama and Kakutani want it to.

The PMC Has Sex

DURING THE SUMMER OF LOVE, vanguardist May 1968ers thought that they invented new and revolutionary ways of experiencing sexual pleasure. They did not. They thought they were the first sexual adventurers in the course of human history. They were not. Sex has always been a messy affair, but during the eighteenth century in Europe, especially but not exclusively in France, the mostly male libertines who took sexual freedom seriously were writing about scientific inquiry into the observable world, the death of God, the worthiness of non-European cultures, and desecrating the sacraments while they flouted Christian morality by living in differing degrees of sin. They were part of a sexual revolution, and they were very conscious of its political consequences.

In the eighteenth century, French libertine literature was filled with anthropomorphized clitorises, detailed accounts of foot fetishes, and deep discussions of the pleasures of anal penetration. The sexual revolutionary to whom we owe many of our progressive ideals about sex is the Marquis de Sade. An aristocratic class traitor and a hopeless sexual deviant, he was a supporter of the French Revolution who spent much of his life in miserable prison cells writing pornography. Adorno and Horkheimer noted that the modern, European demystification of sexual behavior began with Sade's reasoning about human sexuality and its probing, restless search for pleasure. In a remarkable pamphlet, contained in his pornographic novel of ideas *Philosophy in the Boudoir*, he writes, "Frenchmen, try harder if you want to be republicans." Sade argued that the 1789 revolution may have overturned church and monarchy but that it should go farther if it wanted to free the people and seal its abolition of superstition and oppression. Sexual knowledge—that is, knowledge of how to obtain pleasure with one's body and the bodies of others—should be available to all without prejudice. Libertinage, the exercise of absolute sexual freedom on the part of avowed atheists, had been the exclusive purview of aristocrats under the *ancien régime*. Sade wanted sexual freedom for all, and he warned that if the revolutionaries did not overturn the idols of sexual morality and demand sexual freedom for the people, the powers of church and king would lie in wait, ready to overturn the revolutionary achievements of Danton and Robespierre and the French masses who had finally overthrown both king and church. In short, Sade warned of a counterrevolution if the sexual revolution did not take the logic of emancipation to its limit.

In *Philosophy in the Boudoir*, a bright, fifteen-year-old virgin named Eugenie is initiated into the mysteries of erotic pleasure with men and women by an experienced twenty-six-year-old libertine, Madame de Saint-Ange, who teaches her how to "maximize" her pleasure in sex: in the pamphlet within the novel, Sade argues that adultery, sodomy, prostitution, incest, and rape should all be decriminalized. He turned out to be partially prescient. In 2020 in the United States, sex before and outside of marriage is no longer taboo: outside of extreme religious sects, mothers and fathers do not weep about deflowered sons or sexually experienced daughters. Furthermore, homosexuality has been decriminalized in almost every industrialized democracy in the world, while gay marriage has been legalized in many of these countries as well. The normalization or at least decriminalization of prostitution is seen in liberal democracies as a boon for sex workers and a final step in a liberal, sexually enlightened society. It is hard to deny that Sade was a political visionary—in part. Not all of the taboos Sade listed as oppressive have been lifted by enlightened societies. The dark aspect of his sexual enlightenment, the systematic misuse and abuse of others for one's own pleasure, or sadism, for example, has not become socially acceptable in any situation. Sadism was for Theodor Adorno and Max Horkheimer at the end of World War II a philosophical system that justified the radical coldness of the Enlightenment as the rampant instrumentalization and exploitation and abuse of others—workers, chattel, serfs, and slaves. Adorno and Horkheimer argued that eighteenth-century sentimentality was the obverse of sadism. Both value systems were necessary for the expansion of capitalism: do-goodism and good intentions masking a world conquering reduction of life to profit margins.

The sexual revolutionaries of the 1960s replicated in part the Sadean enlightenment, without acknowledging their Western predecessor: they preferred citing Eastern sexual arts in their innovations. The New Left sexual revolutionaries believed that they had forged a new relationship to pleasure that they wanted to share with the world. Just as they rejected the paltry satisfactions and mass-manufactured goods and TV dinners provided by the affluent society, they rejected old-fashioned ways of having intercourse. From the muddy fields of Woodstock to the fragrant groves of Ken Kesey's compound, the counterculture and the New Left proudly experimented with allegedly novel forms of hedonism that most of the time turned into polygamy for one charismatic male and submission of a group of wan women to his will.

Feminists, unhappy with the primal horde antics of New Left men, discovered that women had to take back their own bodies and, in so doing, their relationship to pleasure. When the Boston Women's Health Book Collective published *Our Bodies, Our Selves*, a female-oriented guide to women's health, they promoted the idea that the establishment had been keeping information about female anatomy and female experience from women. They believed that a compilation of critical information shared in networks of women would lead finally to the full emancipation of female sexuality. If the Sadean heroine was liberated by orgasms, PMC feminists believed instead that it was information about achieving orgasms that was truly emancipatory. College-educated New Left women really thought they were at the vanguard of sex and social life. *Our Bodies* suggested that everything a woman did—learning to repair her car, taking a long hike, going kayaking—was a personal leisure activity that contained incredible political significance. *Our Bodies* insisted that women need to understand their bodies because men deny them access to this magical, frightening, unruly thing. The authors were addressing PMC women when they complained about visiting condescending ob-gyns who were visibly impatient to run off to their tennis matches after quick looks down the speculum. The authors overlooked the fact that most women in the world did not receive regular medical care at all. In a further twist on their "privilege," the authors of *Our Bodies* earnestly told women to explore the pleasures of physical labor, ignoring the fact that the majority of women in the world performed physical labor not out of choice but out of necessity. Throughout human history, women have broken their backs carrying water and farming, while nursing their babies, harvesting fields by hand, washing clothes in rivers, and so on. When women lived in homes without electricity or running water, they did the kinds of work necessary to survive in agricultural economies of the sort that college-educated urban and suburban women could not imagine—except as exotic places to visit in their gap years. The Industrial Revolution only created more kinds of work for working-class women, some of it physical, some of it based on fine motor skills, but all of it routinized and punishing in its rhythms of production.

In reaction to the hyperbolic ambitions of the women's movement, conservative culture warriors of the 1970s and 1980s promoted a moral panic about the impending dissolution of marriage and the family. But as time passed, countercultural PMC men and women did not become sexual libertines. In fact, the majority of college-educated Americans abandoned promiscuity and nontraditional romantic arrangements as they became more successful in their professions. They were incentivized to settle down and stop cycling through partners as their incomes and assets increased. The protection of PMC socioeconomic status created opportunities for sacrifice and compromise that precarious working-class people abjured. In 2020, it is among non-college-educated people that we find growing rates of divorce and single parenthood. It is truly an ironic reversal in values, upending the logic of the culture wars when PMC families, whether straight or gay, embrace monogamy and family values with greater zeal than their working-class counterparts.

For PMC feminism, the revolution in sex was mostly a revolution in information and education. It was a revolution that could be made by reading a book, or in a consciousness-raising group about reading that book. It was a revolution that made orgasm and pleasure objects of PMC moral and pedagogical refinement (remember the G spot?). To be part of this revolution, you had to accept that the private experiences and lives of elite PMC people were the most important sites of meaningful political and cultural activity. In sex-positive PMC feminism, the best sex could be had in a social vacuum: it would take place in a comfortable bed with clean sheets, between consenting partners free of economic or social anxiety. In such an optimal situation, a woman could finger her clitoris, labia, or perineum in a leisurely manner, all the while communicating her needs and desires to a sensitive and receptive partner. Good sex became suffused with the logic of information and communication theory upon which ideals of consent are built.

In stark contrast to sexually enlightened PMC people, working-class men and women were represented in popular culture of the 1970s as trapped in misogyny, homophobia, prejudice, and violence, out of touch with their feelings and unable to communicate their erotic needs. For New Left creatives and liberals working in Hollywood in the 1970s, working-class people were living in the sexual dark ages. Working-class men were hopelessly authoritarian and working-class women unwittingly submissive to the patriarchal power of a family wage earner. Whereas at the turn of the nineteenth century, the working class had been undeniably at the vanguard of political struggles against capitalists and their proxies, the PMC after 1968 asserted that it alone was at the vanguard of all revolutions, including and above all the sexual revolution.

Under the Obama administration, the state became intensely involved in the enlightened regulation of sex. From 2008, PMC triumphalism under the well-spoken and well-read president channeled the collective energy of liberals to focus on sex in one of the most important sites of class formation: university campuses, especially elite university campuses. Instrumentalized obsession with sexual violence and sexual excess is an important part of American Puritanism: moral and virtuous superiority in the sexual enlightenment makes up an important part of the countercultural inheritance of the PMC. Rather than focusing on economic malfeasance, an ascendant PMC elite under Obama pursued sexual crimes—not at work or in the workplace but on college campuses—with a zeal that liberals reserve for any policy that diverts attention away from economic redistribution. In short, rather than break up the banks or reform the financial sector after he took office, Obama wanted to use his electoral victory to eliminate sexual violence on college campuses. In 2011, his Department of Education Office for Civil Rights sent a "Dear Colleague" letter to more than seven thousand universities warning them that if they did not take action to prevent and remedy sexual violence and sexual assault on their campuses, they would risk losing their rights to all federal funding. Legal commentators today admit that college administrations reacted to the letter with overcompliance. Many Title IX offices rejected innocent-until-proven-guilty principles that form the democratic rule of law and set up campus investigative panels and bodies that became little more than kangaroo courts.

At the same time, sensational stories of sexual violence and sexual abuse on college campuses emerged in the mainstream media, as if to confirm the necessity of the Obama administration's stringent new policies. In 2015, at the height of the

Obama-era sex panic, Kirby Dick's *The Hunting Ground* was released by—wait for it—the Weinstein Company. Dick's documentary presented college campuses as terrifying places for young women to live. Dick, with the help of Harvey Weinstein, pandered to his liberal audience's thirst for stories about campus sexual violence. In 2016, Amber Frost cited the National Crime Victimization Survey numbers showing that non-college-going women were 1.2 times more likely to be sexually assaulted than their college-going counterparts. Sexual violence on college campuses attracted liberal PMC elites to a new front in the culture wars, far away from inequality, oppression, and workplace sexual harassment and discrimination. Fighting sexual violence on campus allowed the PMC to reinforce its belief that white-collar professionals and lawyers like Atticus Finch were the true heroes in low-risk struggles against anything but economic abuse.

Rolling Stone, a magazine born in the crucible of the rock 'n' roll, drug-fueled, libertine counterculture of San Francisco in 1967, covered one of the most lurid campus sexual violence stories of the Obama era. The magazine was once a highly successful media outlet for the rock 'n' roll–fueled generation of middle-class consumers with growing buying power. By 2014, it had become just another mainstream magazine competing for eyeballs on the internet. The economic crisis of 2008 hit the magazine particularly hard. Ad revenues for print magazines peaked in 2007 and declined steadily year after year, with no respite from either digital sales or the supposed economic "recovery" engineered by the Bush and Obama administrations. It is quite understandable that when contributing editor Sabrina Erdely uncovered the story of an alleged gang rape at the University of Virginia (UVA), Jan Wenner and *Rolling Stone's* editorial board rushed to publish her piece, "Rape on Campus." The nine-thousand-word story detailed from the point of view of "Jackie," the alleged victim, a horrifying gang rape that had taken place at the Phi Beta Kappa Psi fraternity house in 2012. The story got 2.7 million online views on *Rolling Stone's* site, more than any other noncelebrity feature the magazine had ever published. When the *Washington Post* decided to launch an independent investigation into Jackie's story, it became apparent that Erdely had not corroborated any of the details that Jackie had given her. Among the many gaps in Jackie's story, the *Washington Post* reporters discovered that there was no record of a party at the frat house on the night Jackie alleged she was raped. In 2015, the magazine published a retraction of the story along with a detailed forensic investigation into Erdely's journalistic failings performed by a team from the Columbia School of Journalism. *Rolling Stone* and Sabrina Erdely were then sued by the fraternity Phi Beta Kappa Psi and by Nicole Eramo, dean of students at UVA, for defamation. The wider, cultural and political consequences of such a flagrant case of professional failure are difficult to assess, but the Right certainly knew how to inflame popular hatred and resentment of the "mainstream media" and professional journalists and it took full advantage of this flagrant failure in reporting. Far right news site *The Daily Caller* became obsessed with the case and gloated over *Rolling Stone's* and Erdely's disgrace and legal troubles. For the Conservatives and the far right incubators of incel anger, the UVA story confirmed their narrative: liberal media were filled with sensation-seeking hypocrites looking to cash in on fake news stories demonizing young men.

Fifty years after the Summer of Love, college-going women were armed with more information and more sex education than any generation before them, but they seemed less capable of assuming sexual agency and more in need of protection than previous generations of women, who had had to deal with sexual autonomy and male desire without the help of university Title IX officers. For Laura Kipnis, self-described "left-wing feminist," "rebel," and freethinker and professor at Northwestern University, we were living through a new period of sexual paranoia. Kipnis's account of her own Title IX investigation and the case against her former Northwestern colleague Peter Ludlow, make up the heart of her book on this topic, *Unwanted Advances: Sexual Paranoia Comes to Campus*. Kipnis presents a clear, evenhanded account of the Kafkaesque Title IX investigation launched against her after she published a series of articles about Northwestern and Peter Ludlow's case in the *Chronicle of Higher Education*. The first half of Kipnis's book is about the accusations against the philosophy professor and the Title IX investigation that Northwestern launched against both Ludlow and Kipnis herself. Kipnis concludes that section with the observation that even though Ludlow was certainly guilty of inappropriate behavior with an undergraduate and a graduate student, the loss of his job as punishment was entirely incommensurate with his crime, which Kipnis describes as motivated by naive childishness rather than raw abuse and exploitation. In the second half of *Unwanted Advances*, Kipnis summarizes many of the stories of the abuse of Title IX that she heard after going public as the subject of a Title IX investigation herself. For her trouble,

Kipnis became a target of campus feminists and activists, but Kipnis would not be silenced. She is a liberal, a high liberal, which is the very best kind of liberal there is. She believes in robust debate and vigorous public dissent in the university, and her presentation of the abuse of Title IX is a courageous act in the cancel culture demonization of anyone who dares to question the protocols and assumptions behind sexual harassment investigations on college campuses.

For Kipnis, the worst thing about sexual paranoia is that it makes us "dumb." Sex panics provide "a formula for intellectual rigidity." She blames the witch hunt atmosphere on campuses for undermining the traditional ideals of the university—as a refuge for freethinkers, who are now being buried by an "avalanche of platitudes and fear." The ideal university that Kipnis cherishes is a fantasy built on the social ideal of an egalitarian society, where students and professors are libertine-like freethinkers, free of material want. While this ideal was operative between 1945 and 1972, intensifying inequality and the increasing cost of higher education have destroyed this mid-century American idea of the university. In Kipnis's fantasy university, everyone lives in the affluent society: therein lies the basis of her ideal of intellectual freedom. Kipnis came of age at the tail end of an unprecedented expansion of higher education in the United States, and she exudes the confidence and bravado of someone who has not known real professional or economic insecurity. She is remarkably cut off from the torture chamber buzz of anxiety that afflicts students today. She gives sexual paranoia too much credit for the intellectual torpor of contemporary university life: in my experience, professional and economic insecurity is the greatest thought inhibitor of all.

In concluding *Unwanted Advances*, Kipnis presents a cogent analysis of an epidemic of college blackout drinking while presenting the moral panic of our times as related to the incomplete emancipation of female sexuality. She believes that the problems of campus sex can be solved with more education for men and women on the topic of sexual ambivalence, consent, and agency. What if overvaluation of information and "education" is actually part of the problem with coming of age under neoliberalism and its austerity policies? What if competition for places at institutions of higher education and the higher and higher barrier of entry to the PMC are actually what fuels the sex panics that make us all more stupid? In a society that sees education as a private good, an asset to be used to compete in an increasingly precarious and uncertain world, most young people do not feel as if they can afford to be curious or pleasure seeking while in college. The intellectual and erotic freedoms cherished by Kipnis are shaped by a kind of aristocratic libertine thought enabled by mid-century American principles of economic redistribution and equality that contemporary university administrations neither understand nor support.

The Obama administration's zealous enforcement of Title IX is very different from the way in which Hank Paulson and Timothy Geithner engineered the bailout of criminal financial institutions after the financial meltdown of 2008. Why didn't the Obama administration send a "Dear Colleague" letter to investment bankers and financial advisors, warning them about helping their clients evade billions of dollars in taxes, taxes that used correctly could be reinvested in public universities and public education programs? What about a "Dear Colleague" letter addressed to Big Pharma, warning it about federal regulations coming down the pipeline about opioid dumping in rural areas? What about a "Dear Colleague" letter addressed to Wells Fargo, Goldman Sachs, AIG, JP Morgan Chase, Bank of America, or any other institution that insured, sold, and packaged bad mortgages to the detriment of borrowers and investors? What about "Dear Colleague" letters to fossil fuel companies warning them about their cover-up about their knowledge of carbon production and climate change? In the absence of such letters, we have to conclude that PMC elites prefer fomenting moral panics to implementing even the most modest redistributive or progressive economic policies, even after a global financial catastrophe.

To close out our discussion of campus sex panics, we have to turn to the story of Emma Sulkowicz. In 2015, Sulkowicz graduated from Columbia University with a BA in visual arts, for which her performance *Mattress Performance: Carry That Weight* fulfilled a degree requirement. Sulkowicz's piece was staged as a protest and "performance" against the fact that her 2013 allegations of rape against fellow undergraduate Paul Nungesser had not led to any consequences for him and that he was allowed to continue being a student at Columbia. Sulkowicz had wanted him expelled for the alleged attack, but after an internal inquiry, Columbia University found Nungesser without responsibility for the alleged assault. Sulkowicz was furious about the findings, and she spent her senior year on the campus carrying the mattress upon which the alleged violation took place. Sulkowicz's sense of revanchist entitlement, her confident disregard for due process (the centerpiece of liberalism's rule of law), her indifference to privacy—of her alleged attacker and her own—became realized in her "performance" as art.

Like all endurance-based performance art, the senseless expenditure of physical effort is a display of the elites' absolute freedom from the necessity of physical labor. From this point of view, Sulkowicz's performance of mattress carrying makes a mockery of the physicality of manual labor. Most workers in the world still labor with their bodies and have to endure physical pain and hardship during a day's work: to "choose" physical endurance is the ultimate sign of PMC sovereignty. It should go without saying that Sulkowicz first and foremost objectified her own trauma. The performance allowed her a degree of dissociation, but it also gave her the platform upon which to make a bid for visibility, notoriety, fame, and celebrity. She became a one-woman placard, publicizing a traumatic experience to make public something she had to endure in private. Sulkowicz as an artist, and a child of PMC elites (her parents are successful business psychologists in Manhattan), was responding to, commenting on, and reproducing the regime of postindustrial work, a kind of work that entails the constant production of publicity-garnering activity in the name of self-branding. In the pursuit of justice, Sulkowicz became famous for her ability to turn private pain into public spectacle.

One of the most notorious artists of the internet age, Ryan Trecartin also works on new media celebrity by staging performances of crazy parties gone wrong and gone wild. His video performances are carnivalesque, nonsensical, drug-addled events characterized by generalized dissolution, abjection, and thwarted pleasure seeking. Trecartin advertises himself as self-taught, campy, messy, and working class. Sulkowicz's art partook of the craving for fame that animates all of Trecartin's work, but she had a different aim in advertising her traumatic sexual experiences: her art was made out of her frustration about Nungesser's impunity. After graduating from Columbia, Sulkowicz was admitted into the highly selective Whitney Program, a year-long residency for art stars in the making, and her follow-up artistic work continued on the register of sexual sensationalism and art world prestige economy anxiety: she began with *Ceci n'est pas un viol* (This is not a rape), a video restaging of her rape. She also had herself tied up by an S&M professional she called "Mr. Whitney" while she wore a white bikini emblazoned with a W and an M, standing for, we assume, "Whitney Museum." Her inane personal statements about her work parrot the tired truisms about female empowerment and the need to counter criticism of "fem bodies."

Hailed by both performance artist Marina Abramovic and *New York Times* art critic Roberta Smith as a genius, Sulkowicz proved ambivalent about her art world success. In 2017, she did a performance piece as a therapist at the fake Healing Touch Integral Wellness Center in Philadelphia. *Bustle* magazine praised her new work for resisting Trump.

But then, two years later, in 2019, she was featured in the *Cut* hanging around alt-light, men's rights types who were once her biggest haters online. Sulkowicz claimed that she had become open to their point of view. She also claimed to be tired of contemporary art and said that she was quitting being an artist. In the meantime, her alleged attacker, Paul Nungesser, and Columbia University settled out of court a lawsuit in which Nungesser successfully sued the university for gender discrimination based on Title IX. For liberals, sexual violence on campus is of critical importance because (1) universities are sites of class reproduction, and all intersubjective encounters in such places must be rationalized, and (2) the PMC elite loves to play the virtuous hero in clear-cut moral dramas where economic exploitation is not an issue. Laura Kipnis should not have been surprised by the fact that a segment of PMC young people no longer sees sex as an activity where pleasure and agency are critical. For Emma Sulkowicz, everything that happens to her can be instrumentalized and turned into fodder for publicity and prosecution. The lack of boundaries between the personal and the political is the poisoned fruit of contemporary neoliberalism's metabolization of the historical counterculture.

If the case of Harvey Weinstein lies outside of the purview of my critique of sex panics, it is because Jodi Kantor and Megan Twohey focused on workplace sexual assault, corroborated by countless victims and employees of the former movie mogul. It would be wonderful if we could extend the investigative attention and care paid to Harvey Weinstein's victims to other workers who have been exploited and abused in far less glamorous workplaces. In Kantor and Twohey's reporting, Weinstein's victims were terrified of him because of the power he wielded over their careers and professional prospects. It is clear that sexual coercion and economic insecurity work together to create conditions for abuse. There is no sexual freedom or pleasure without freedom from the terrifying economic fear for simple survival to which so many of us are reduced. Weinstein's Sadean treatment of women would not have been possible without the professional and economic power that he wielded over an entire industry. Kipnis, like Sade, believes in a world of sexual adventure without economic coercion— that world is certainly desirable but not realizable under the current conditions wrought by capitalism and its narrowing spaces of authentic intersubjective experience.

Every Child Needs the Good Enough State
The richness of childhood needs to be embraced as a social good

It took the devastation of the Civil War to establish government provision for veterans and their kin. Panic about childhood and its inviolability along with a collective sense of responsibility for soldiers, widows, and their children intensified at the end of World War I. Mass immigration, industrialization, and financial crises also cast new light on collective responsibility for the suering and deprivation of society's most vulnerable. Agitators such as Jane Addams and Eugene V. Debs led movements demanding social services and publicly funded welfare for working people.

Beyond just capitalists, workers faced a new class of antagonists at the new century's dawn: bosses, engineers, experts, and advertisers. In their 1976 essay, "The Professional Managerial Class," Barbara and John Ehrenreich defined the salient qualities of this intermediary class, between the proletariat and the capitalist, who advocated for wealth redistribution while decrying working-class consumption habits. Their role in the class war was not obvious in the Progressive Era, but the pmc began to serve capital by pioneering new forms of cultural discipline and reinforcing the social order. With complete faith in their position as arbiters of morality, the pmc established cultural norms that would shape American childrearing for generations.

Benjamin Spock was one of the most influential figures of this new class. Popularizing psychoanalytic ideas about pleasure and identification, Spock played an important role in the formation of new pmc identities. In his best seller, *Baby and Child Care*, first published in 1945— just as the first boomers began to toddle—Spock advised new parents that they should trust themselves with their babies. While the naturalness and intuition that Spock praised seemed like an antidote to authoritarian baby care, his readers were squarely positioned as mid-century consumers seeking assurance and "empowerment" through the consumption of new ideas about child development.

Breaking with family traditions of austerity and infant discipline, the newly prosperous American parent/consumer of advice distinguished herself from previous generations and working-class people by embracing expert advice. Even though Spock warned parents of both old-fashioned and faddish childrearing counsel, he still packaged his ideas in an attractive book that has sometimes been hailed as the American twentieth century's second-best seller, after the Bible. Even at the height of his New Left activism, and while under attack for his countercultural sympathies, his critics never failed to call him doctor. Dr Spock emphasized the PMC love of professional credentialism even while he reminded his readers relentlessly that they were the ones in the know. "You can read books and articles, but the main way you will learn is to be observant in a meaningful way. That means spending time, looking and listening to your baby, not just feeding and cleaning him . . . and then trusting yourself. Because you do know more than you think you do."

In the 1970s, as budding PMC boomers dabbled in self-indulgent experiments with "Eastern" religions and privileged self-expression over family ties, they looked at their blue-collar brethren as backward traditionalists. Today, the situation appears reversed. Historians and sociologists like Jeerson Cowie and Jennifer Silva have shown that working-class Americans today have more unstable family lives and greater instances of divorce and single parenthood than their PMC counterparts. After four decades of capitalist attack, working-class families and kinship networks are at a breaking point. Facing layoffs and evictions, workers find it almost impossible to establish continuity of relationships and stable kinship ties.

In the meantime, college-educated Americans are far more likely to marry and remain married within their class. In the past fifty years, the PMC family has become a veritable redoubt from which class privilege is reproduced. From the very moment of conception, which for PMC parents is a "choice," optimization of children and their "potential" has become a torturous preoccupation. The 40 percent of American children conceived outside of marriage are deemed unworthy of collective attention or public concern. It is not an exaggeration to say that the reproduction of class privilege, or as the Ehrenreichs put it, "the maintenance of order," is being played out in the configuration of childhood itself.

Paula Fass identifies fear as one of the distinctive features of contemporary middle-class parenting as "[middle-class parents] imagine what an unsuccessful child might face in the future." In her best seller, *Perfect Madness: Motherhood in an Age of Anxiety*, Judith Warner decries the anguished, competitive perfectionism of contemporary professional-class motherhood. Since 2006, when Warner published her book, the anxiety of parenthood has only intensified. *Jacobin* editor Megan Erickson argues that these anxieties and fears are not unjustified, "given the increasing stratification even within the top 1 percent of the country's earners as the 2008–2009 financial crisis has only exacerbated the class war that those on top wage against all those below them." Parenting fads like "infant education" have become hot commodities in a society where economic polarization and a collapse of public institutions and goods undermine the well-being of dependents and their caregivers.

> "Parental anxiety begins early for the wealthiest parents, but their faith in parenting fads and technology are inflamed by start-ups and venture capitalists."

Perfectionist PMC parents are crusading class-formation pioneers: they will not hesitate to humiliate nannies, babysitters, teachers, grandmothers, and other parents about the horrific effects of vaccines, screen time, tickling, dolls with faces, cigarette-shaped candy, or sugar in general. For their children, they model social superiority and utter indifference to the experiences of others.

Parental anxiety begins early for the wealthiest parents, but their PMC faith in parenting fads and technology are inflamed by start-ups and venture capitalists. Take, for instance, the National Institutes of Health (NIH)–funded development of the Owlet Smart Sock. A baby sock designed to monitor your baby's heartbeat and oxygen levels while she is sleeping, the Smart Sock collects a constant stream of data about your bundle of joy and sends an alert to your smartphone if any of her measurements appear abnormal. In 2012, Owlet received $3 million from the NIH as well as $25 million of private equity and venture-capital funding, as the government and investors all risibly claimed to be interested in improving US infant health. Obama-era federal programs were so enamored with entrepreneurialism that the NIH was willing to back the Orwellian idea of the "connected nursery" with taxpayer dollars.

Smart Socks or no, should we be so worried about infant health outcomes? A quick glance at World Bank data on under-five infant mortality shows that there has been a dramatic global decline in this area in the past fifty years. Thanks to the successful implementation of polio and smallpox vaccines and other advances, early childhood deaths have diminished from 93.4 per 1,000 live births in 1960 to 40.8 in 2016.In the United States, the decrease is just as dramatic, with 30 deaths per 1,000 live births in 1960 to 6.5 today — with no help from the Owlet Smart Sock at all.

So, what in fact does the Owlet gadget do other than attract grant money and venture-capital investment? It cuts communication between parents and babies; the most carnal and demanding of human relationships is reduced to a bitter cocktail of anxiety and information. "Owlet" babies are strangely unable to demand the care that they need: a sensor, an app, and a smartphone must be activated to alert parents to a baby's needs. As the gulf between rich and poor has widened, and social mobility has decreased in every ethnic group, the PMC home has become a laboratory of increasingly lavish and expensive childcare equipment and demanding child-rearing techniques.

The class war from above has had dire consequences for all American children and their caretakers, but the toll it has taken on the poorest families is staggering. Recently, the Urban Institute found that children are the poorest segment of American society, with 22 percent living in poverty and 38.8 percent having experienced some form of poverty in their lives. The numbers for African-American children are even more dire: 38.8 percent of black children living in poverty and 75.4 percent have lived in poverty.

> "The unglamorous infrastructure of good enough parenting is the good enough state, a social-democratic system of redistributive support."

While PMC parenting fads promote extraordinary caretaking techniques, D. W. Winnicott praised ordinary devoted mothers for bonding with their infants in a way that gave an astonishing number of people the mental health to access play, creativity, and richness of experience. Winnicott had a very expansive, non-gendered idea of the caretaker; however, for the sake of brevity, I use his term the "good enough mother," in discussing his ideas. The "good enough mother" is based on her imperfect responses to her baby's needs: early adaptation to newborn dependency is intense, but a good enough mother adapts to her baby's growing physical and emotional capacity to endure frustration by failing to respond to the baby's demands immediately. These necessary failures reflect the mother's absorption in other tasks and represent opportunities for the baby to establish a healthy tolerance for frustration and recognition of self and other. Winnicott's most famous case study, described in *Holding and Interpretation*, analyzes a man incapable of spontaneity or excitement, whose mother, rather than identifying with the infant, had tried to be "perfect" in her infant-care routines.

In his introduction to *The Child, The Family, and the Outside World*, published in 1964, Winnicott writes,

> I am trying to draw attention to the immense contribution to the individual and the society which the ordinary good mother with her husband in support makes at the beginning, and which she does simply through being devoted to her infant. Is not this contribution of the devoted mother unrecognized precisely because it is immense? If this contribution is accepted it follows that everyone who is sane, everyone feels himself to be a person in the world, and for whom the world means something, every happy person, is in infinite debt to a woman . . . [T]he result of such recognition of the maternal role . . . will not be gratitude or even praise. The result will be a lessening in ourselves of a fear. If our society delays making full acknowledgment of this dependence which is a historical fact in the initial stage of development in every individual, there must remain a block to ease and complete health, a block that comes from a fear.

In postwar Great Britain, Winnicott welcomed the redistribution of social surplus that would allow the greatest number of Britons to experience the richness and health of his own privileged childhood. That childhood allowed him to expand on his ability for observation, empathy, and play — qualities every baby deserves to enjoy.

Though it is difficult to imagine a time when the richness of childhood experience was embraced as a public good, it was only fifty years ago that Winnicott's psychoanalytic theories were founded on the idea of collective and mutual responsibility for dependents and their caretakers. The unglamorous infrastructural support of good enough parenting is the good enough state, a social-democratic system of redistributive support.

If the good enough mother can be cherished as cultural inheritance and a social good, we can begin to build a society where dependency is not feared or demonized. We can begin to build a world where no child will ever be "trained" or "fine-tuned" to "succeed" or "excel." We will be able to imagine a world where playfulness and the environments that support it will be prioritized when we decide how to redistribute the social surplus. We will be able to imagine a world where a baby communicates beautifully with her devoted caretaker because he has the time and space to be absorbed from her first hour, in the richness of the infant's expanding world.

The Apotheosis of the Professional Class

By 2019, more than one-third of Americans over the age of twenty-five had a college degree, the highest proportion in US history. The professional-managerial class (PMC) has made the bachelor's degree a necessary credential for anyone who wants to enter its ranks.

In colleges, especially small liberal arts colleges, students are learning the language of identity protocols and its ancillary politics, and they are able to exercise their sense of entitlement to forms of social interaction that enable them to function in and dominate the liberal professions. In the meantime, liberal leaders find it all the more easy to dismiss the 64 percent of Americans who fail to earn that degree as backward and guilty of the societal ills that the PMC has individualized, psychologized, and managed.

If the majority of Americans do not attend college, the majority of college students in the United States do not attend private liberal arts colleges: public universities do most of the work of educating students, but we rarely hear about their individual attendees. They are the masses, unnamed and faceless, often evoked in images of spring breakers gone wild, or football fans dressed in Buckeyes regalia. In the popular media and in the popular imagination, attendees of small liberal arts colleges appear as individuals who are culturally significant, if sometimes more spoiled than your average twenty-year-old. What happens in private colleges takes on outsize importance, because these institutions are the training grounds for elite members of the PMC.

Liberal contempt for the "masses" and media fetishism of what goes on at elite private universities and colleges have shaped reporting on recent events at Smith College, a women's school that is nearly 150 years old, roiled by struggles over its management of conflicts shaped by social media, class, and race. In July 2018, a student at Smith leveled accusations of racism against members of staff after being questioned by a campus security officer about her presence in a building that was meant to be closed.

On social media, she publicly identified the janitor who allegedly alerted security to her presence and two staff members who had nothing to do with this incident, branding them as racists. Her story about being racially profiled while eating lunch and minding her own business attracted attention from the national media, and Smith College officials promised speedy action to combat racism on campus.

Unexpectedly, an independent investigation commissioned by the college found no evidence of wrongdoing or racial bias on the part of the accused staff. However, the college administration still pressed them to take part in "restorative" processes that implied they were guilty of an offense. Behind the focus on race in the public discourse around the incident lurked another story about class privilege and social and economic disadvantage.

THE LIBERAL ARTS COMPLEX

The 2018 incident at Smith College is broadly representative of what is happening at other private institutions located in rural areas of the Northeast, such as Haverford, Amherst, Williams, and Wellesley. These colleges have become laboratories of PMC culture, drawing well-educated students from both private high schools and academically excellent public high schools. Like its competitors, Smith has worked hard to diversify its student body and, to a lesser extent, its faculty. Smith has attempted to forge its ideals of equity, diversity, and inclusion in colonial-era buildings and idyllic quadrangles behind ivy-covered walls. But its very location vitiates such efforts.

Smith, like many other elite liberal arts colleges, has become an island of cosmopolitanism, diversity, and prosperity in an area that, along with most of rural America, has suffered decades of economic stagnation. In 2019, Northampton's unemployment rate was twice that of Boston's, and its economy is reliant on tourism and education. Colleges like Smith, like any other institution, employ blue-collar and union workers to clean and repair their quaint facilities or to serve their student body food in cafeterias.

Smith draws on the local employment pool to staff its lower-level administrative positions that guarantee the smooth running of its bureaucracy. Good management of a college's resources means paying these sorts of workers as little as you can get away with while rewarding famous professors and upper-level administrators to the greatest possible extent. Unfortunately for the administration of the colleges, they cannot curate their working-class employees, who, unlike the PMC bosses and the PMC-aspiring student body, often remain bound to their places of birth, notoriously rooted in communities and families that allow them to survive on almost poverty wages.

Despite increasing rates of college enrollment in the United States, economic mobility for the majority of Americans has stagnated over the past fifty years. The costs of higher education have become increasingly privatized, as generations of American college students now labor under the burden of unpayable student loan debt. An educated populace is a public good and a necessary condition for democracy. However, the expansion of college education has not led to a dramatic improvement in the quality of debate in the American public sphere. We are caught between two poles, as right-wing media outlets like Fox News, on the one hand, flirt with conspiracist thinking and trade in rage, suspicion, and xenophobia, while the likes of MSNBC and CNN compete in moral panics and PMC virtue hoarding, on the other.

We might even argue that the combination of increasing economic inequality and the growth of college participation has produced a divided and obdurately suspicious polity. An economic system of inequality has exacerbated disparities, enabled by the meritocracy and its secular moral code of liberalism that PMC elites have redefined to suit their own material and psychological needs. The ideal of education as a driver of social mobility is a fantasy that keeps a corrupt meritocracy creaking along, an institution broadly recognized as fatally flawed and unfit for the task of distributing education as a public good.

As levels of educational attainment have increased along with inequality, the lure of admission to the most prestigious colleges and universities has grown stronger. A degree from an elite private college is supposed to be a marker of indelible distinction that will stay with the graduate for life. Of the Americans with college degrees, 4 percent have attended private liberal arts colleges. In total, students and graduates from small liberal arts colleges comprise about 1 to 1.5 percent of all Americans. Even in this rarefied sector of higher education, stratification and the hoarding of prestige and capital is opening up a pitiless divide between wealthier and poorer institutions. While schools like Smith have seen their already massive endowments balloon during the pandemic and under an ebullient stock market, Ithaca College is looking to lay off 20 percent of its faculty.

IDEALS AND REALITIES

Those who attend institutions like Smith, Amherst, and Williams may not all hail from the nation's wealthiest 1 percent, but they constitute a very special part of the college-going population. In beautiful, rural settings, they enjoy intense personal attention from professors who are also graduates of elite institutions. In their small classes, students should be able to receive, in isolation from the pressures of family, profession, and market, a well-rounded education in skepticism, curiosity, critical thinking, and general knowledge. This Socratic training comes with the added bonus of strong networking and social bonds with classmates and alumni alike. For these rewards, ambitious students and their families do not balk at the sky-high tuition and fees, which at Smith are close to $80,000 per year. Smith boasts that 58 percent of its students enjoy financial aid. Why not simply lower the tuition? Elite private education has become a luxury good and an important site of philanthropic activity. Just as you wouldn't want to lower the price of a luxury item like a Hermès bag or a Gucci coat, private colleges play the high price/discount game with which consumers of late capitalism's fake deals are all too familiar. "Supporting" worthy students is a philanthropic activity that the college's development officers can sell to wealthy donors for tax deductible donations.

Of course, the realities supported by Smith alumnae, hovering behind the ideal of liberal arts education, are deeply racist and imperialist. Smith alumna Nancy Reagan launched her "Just Say No" propaganda campaign for the War on Drugs while her husband, Ronald Reagan, dismantled the welfare state, deregulated the American media, undermined union power, demonized working-class African Americans, and ignored the AIDS epidemic.

Until the COVID-19 pandemic, colleges like Smith saw rising numbers of applications, reaching an all-time high in 2018, with 5,780 applicants.5 In 2020, Smith's endowment reached $1.9 billion, or $638,000 per student. October 2020 brought the biggest gift in the college's history into its coffers: $50 million.6 These numbers are benchmarks of success for its Yale-educated president, Kathleen

McCartney, who left her position as dean of the Harvard Graduate School of Education to assume leadership of the college in 2013. According to the latest Chronicle of Higher Education numbers, McCartney's executive compensation package totals $720,690 a year.7

Although McCartney has a PhD in psychology and a distinguished academic career, she is, like most contemporary college leaders, preoccupied with fundraising. In addition, following national trends, she has focused on redefining the liberal arts mission of Smith to suit the needs of students who are more pragmatic about their majors, as well as the culture of start-ups and businesses that want to see innovation and entrepreneurship touted in academic mission statements throughout American higher education. On her Smith webpage, McCartney predictably declares a deep affection for innovation and entrepreneurship as core elements of the Smith education. She is also committed to helping Smith women succeed in the C-suite.8 Today, 46.7 percent of Smith undergraduates are majoring in math and science — a number that has steadily increased under McCartney's watch.

McCartney was really engaged in defending a liberal ideal of education, not to mention academic freedom and professional research protocols, that would put her in conflict with the interests of capital represented by Smith's donors and the corporations looking to hire ambitious young women who graduate from the school. Instead, she and Smith tout leadership as a quality the college promotes and nurtures: Is the BA in essence the new MBA? PMC university administrators have covertly merged their language, outlook, and institutional mission statements with the interests of wealthy donors and business leaders.

"Leadership," as a quality promoted by colleges and universities, is simply a code word for compliance with business needs — if we think of classical leadership qualities in literature and history, we find a set of traits highly incompatible with neoliberal institutions. Ruthlessness, love of power, charisma, a willingness to sacrifice others and the self, stoicism, skepticism, decisiveness, cunning, and single-mindedness are all qualities shared by fictional and historical leaders, from Napoleon and Catherine the Great to Odysseus, Genghis Khan, and Julius Caesar, to Joan of Arc, Andrew Carnegie, and Abraham Lincoln.

When a college or university administrator speaks of leadership as a value they want to inculcate in their students, they are more likely referring to the examples of Jack Welch, the CEO who downsized General Electric, or Elizabeth Holmes, founder of the failed start-up Theranos, a young woman who convinced investors that she had invented a revolutionary method of rapidly testing blood using shockingly small blood samples. Like Adam Neumann, deposed CEO of WeWork, her leadership qualities and ability to deceive people grossed her hundreds of millions, if not billions, of dollars.

A NEW REGIME

What does an institution like Smith do when its mission, once grounded in flawed but non-market-driven liberal arts ideals, do when it has completely surrendered to the demands of the C-suite?

It adopts a language of social justice, inclusion, diversity, and equity that no human resources manager from Morgan Stanley, Citibank, or ExxonMobil would find offensive. If the pre-woke workplace was filled with sexism, racism, and overtly punitive evaluation protocols that encouraged the promotion of networked white male employees, the contemporary workplace has evolved into an experimental site of surveillance and retraining, all in the name of employer reputation washing.

Kathleen McCartney's handling of the 2018 incident of alleged racial profiling dramatizes this process in stark detail. The aftermath of the incident has resulted in mandatory anti-racism training for Smith staff, whose average salary is $43,000, and the establishment of affinity dormitories where "students of color and Black students" can choose to live.9 Even though employee training has repeatedly been proven ineffective at preventing bias or harassment in the workplace, employers across the United States are investing in such training against sexual harassment and racism in order to deal with issues of legal compliance and liability while also flashing the badge of the enlightened and the bias-free. In reserving dormitories for students of color, forty years after federally mandated desegregation of public schools and housing, the Smith administration is effectively admitting to having fostered such a racially hostile environment that students of color have to shield themselves from it by residing separately.

Meanwhile, in the classrooms and across campus, students imbibe a culture of extraordinary privilege, not just economically but psychologically. Their every need is catered to and their every thought validated by their professors, who are at their beck and call — so much so that tenure is effectively determined by student assessments of professors' "performance." It is a culture in which the language of social justice is ubiquitous but the ability to distinguish between slights and annoyances, on the one hand, and genuine social oppression, on the other, is quietly extinguished. Whereas earlier generations of students at these elite colleges were openly socialized into taking their place among the ruling elite, the current crop is trained to perform that function while draping it in the language of affirmation, empowerment, and justice. And the emerging multicultural cohort of managers and influencers use their social justice portfolio to great effect as they climb their way up the PMC career ladder.

All these aspects of college culture were on display in the alleged racial profiling incident of July 31, 2018. It attracted national coverage after Smith sophomore Oumou Kanoute posted about it on her Facebook page, picked up by national news outlets including CNN, the New York Times, and the Washington Post, which emphasized Kanoute's trauma in their reporting.11 In her Facebook post, Kanoute stated that she was having lunch and relaxing in the living area of Smith's Tyler House when someone called campus police on her. She described being observed by a man and a woman before the police arrived, testifying that they were pacing a room away from her, agitated by her very presence.

When a campus security officer finally arrived and approached her, accompanied by a janitor, they questioned her right to be where she was.

Kanoute reported being deeply traumatized after the incident, afraid to go to sleep in her room and unable to resume normal life on campus:

All I did was be black. It's outrageous that some people question my being at Smith ... No student of color should have to explain why they belong at prestigious white institutions. I worked my hardest to get into Smith, and I deserve to feel safe on my campus.

In response to the Facebook post, McCartney addressed a public apology to Kanoute and promptly suspended the janitor involved in the incident.12 None of the immediate reporting raised any questions about McCartney's apology or the worker's suspension.

Kanoute herself referred to him in social media posts as a "racist punk." The Washington Post quoted Phillip Atiba Goff, president of the Center for Policing Equity: "The issue is that, for many folks, law enforcement has been seen as their own racism valet."13 The description implies that the Smith janitor was behaving like an entitled aristocrat or boss, calling upon police to govern the campus according to his racist views. The story appeared to confirm liberal suspicions about a toxic and deeply entrenched strain of racism and a culture of fear and resentment among working-class whites, including those working low-paying jobs at small liberal arts colleges — people whose racism is so irrational and inescapable that they are willing to jeopardize their livelihoods when they act on their alleged white supremacy.

INVESTIGATING THE STORY

As mentioned earlier, there was an afterword to the incident:

Smith commissioned an independent third-party investigation of the events on July 31, 2018. The report found no evidence that any Smith employee had behaved improperly.14 Major news outlets ignored that report upon its public release in October 2018, although Emma Whitford at Inside Higher Ed published a piece on it.15 Whitford reported that the Sanghavi Law Office hired by Smith had discovered no evidence that the suspended employee was motivated by racial bias, while noting that many Smith alumnae and students had denounced the report's findings on social media. The American Civil Liberties Union, which had begun representing Kanoute, also condemned the report.

The investigators interviewed the "Caller," who remained unnamed, and Tyler Hall cafeteria worker Jackie Blair, with whom Kanoute had a brief exchange on the day of the incident, in the presence of their union representatives. The report made public the nature of the exchange between Kanoute and Blair, who had served Kanoute food before the incident, as well as the exchange between Kanoute, the janitor, and the police officer. The janitor, who was in his sixties, made a mistake when he called campus police that day: Kanoute was right to assert that he could have come over to talk to her before doing so. However, the police officer was not armed, as she had claimed. His recorded interaction with her was polite and apologetic.

In February 2021, the New York Times published a lengthy investigation of the incident by Michael Powell.17 Conservative figures took up the plight of the working-class people involved in the drama, two of whom Kanoute named in subsequent Facebook posts. In the NYT opinion pages, Bret Stephens accused the liberal left of capitulating to the "Woke left." In March 2021, conservative African American leaders from a group called 1776 Unites penned an open letter to Smith, condemning McCartney's handling of the incident:

> Many of us participated in the Civil Rights movement, fighting for equal treatment under the law, which included due process and the presumption of innocence. We didn't march so that Americans of any race could be presumed guilty and punished for false accusations while the elite institution that employed them cowered in fear of a social media mob. We certainly didn't march so that privileged Blacks could abuse working class whites based on "lived experience."

McCartney had said in her apologies to the student that she accepted Kanoute's account of what happened based on the category of "lived experience."

As an addendum — or a sideshow, depending on your point of view — one former Smith employee, Jodi Shaw, created a smallscale media furor. Following the July 2018 incident, Shaw refused to talk about race during mandatory anti-racism training, then quit her position as a student support coordinator and publicly denounced Smith as a workplace hostile to its white employees.

She found support in right-wing circles and published an open letter to Kathleen McCartney on the Substack of conservative provocateur Bari Weiss, while articulating grandiose hopes for "change" on her own YouTube channel. Shaw, a single mother of two, also started a GoFundMe page that has attracted over $200,000 in donations. She styles herself as a voice for Smith employees who are afraid to speak up against McCartney's administration. Shaw is a Smith alumna, and when she quit her job, she was making $45,000 a year. While she may have rejected the invasiveness of Smith's anti-bias training, she's no working-class heroine. Her YouTube videos and written denunciations of Smith's anti-white culture are filled with familiar PMC-engineered clichés about visibility, social change, victimhood, and representation.

Like McCartney, Shaw wants the public and her community to believe that she is operating on behalf of the rights of white workers at Smith. She refers to giving voice to those silenced by Smith's workplace culture, but while she may seem delusional and reactionary, we should judge McCartney just as harshly for her equally far-fetched claims. In apologizing to Kanoute and asserting that the student belongs "in all Smith spaces," she claims that her administration is building "an inclusive, diverse and sustainable community ... Members of the Smith campus community share a responsibility to ensure that each of us is safe and each of us is treated with respect."21 By repeating the word "community" over and over again, McCartney hopes to cast away the unequal reality of the employer/employee relationship that defines her antagonism toward the janitor she put on administrative leave on the basis of a student's Facebook post.

McCartney may have displayed the leadership qualities necessary to guarantee her bona fides as a neoliberal boss, ready to treat her employees as guilty before proven innocent, but she wants her peers and her students to see her as an enlightened college president who is on the side of those fighting against a racist society. Her willingness to sacrifice workers on the altar of liberal anti-racism, based merely on the word of an unhappy student, is another sign of her obdurate class identity. I have shown elsewhere that PMC elites have a habit of scapegoating poor whites for the sins of a racist society

Liberalism once touted the presumption of innocence and a general skepticism as markers of its superiority to totalitarian regimes like its much-despised adversaries in the Soviet Union and the People's Republic of China. Today's PMC leaders are eager to embrace an entirely fictious and antisocial form of virtue with disregard for due process and reason, all in the name of narcissistic self-preservation in the face of evidence of their lack of judgment and integrity. I do not expect the president of a small liberal arts college to be a socialist or even a progressive, but I am genuinely surprised at McCartney's utter lack of commitment to the very values of due process and fact-finding that a college like Smith claims to defend and uphold.

Jodi Shaw is now relying on social media celebrity and a lawsuit against Smith to guarantee her livelihood: McCartney took a pay cut during the pandemic but otherwise occupies her office unmolested and unbothered by her abuse of power and her errors in judgment. The leadership cadre to which she belongs is ultimately very forgiving of those in positions of power. McCartney showed herself willing to defend the meritocratic line that the best educated and most well paid among us can, in sacrificing any relationship to material truths, maintain positions of authority and coercion over a myriad of underlings they like to call "members of their community."

"DON'T LET A RICH STUDENT REPORT YOU"

Mark Patenaude was one of two Smith employees misidentified by Kanoute on Facebook as having called the police on her. He told the New York Times: "We used to joke, don't let a rich student report you, because if you do, you're gone." That joke is one of the few accurate things that have been said about employee-student-administration relationships at Smith in all the discourse around the 2018 incident. While manufacturing jobs have disappeared from New England, postindustrial service work has expanded, with a feminized workforce doing the labor of maintaining the American prestige economy, supporting liberal professions and the culture industry. In the postindustrial workplace, where service is key, worker discipline takes the form of constant surveillance by customers and technology.

While Karl Marx described the factory as the infernal site of worker exploitation and coercion, postindustrial workplaces are supposed to provide weightless, frictionless experiences, from oneclick shopping to liberal arts educations that erase the presence of the human worker. The coercive power of labor, in its rawest forms, is increasingly disguised by the language of "woke" management and human resources. If McCartney and Kanoute are aligned, it is because they are willing to treat as guilty and discipline the least respected and lowest paid workers at Smith College.

Sociologist Arlie Hochschild analyzed this regime of affectual self-management in her book The Managed Heart, a study of flight attendants and bill collectors. Hochschild emphasizes that the presentation of the correct attitude is a critical element in postindustrial service work. Patenaude describes an environment in which a cafeteria or janitorial worker at Smith must not only do their job well but must also produce the appropriate attitude of service toward students — or risk being denounced and fired.

Kanoute also named Blair, the cafeteria worker, as a Smith employee who had participated in racial profiling. Blair was in Tyler Hall that day, serving food. She had a brief exchange with Kanoute about access to the dining hall during summer, when it was reserved for teenagers attending a camp. All calls to campus police are recorded, so it is beyond dispute that Blair did not call the police, while Patenaude was not working at the time of the call.

After Kanoute's post appeared, wrongly naming her as the caller, Blair received phone calls at her home telling her she "didn't deserve to live," and found notes taped to her car declaring her a"racist." Although she was not guilty of any wrongdoing, Smith administration urged Blair to go into mediation with Kanoute. She refused. In a message to the Smith community in August 2018, McCartney evoked the concepts of "restorative justice ...willing apology, forgiveness and reconciliation," in reference to the incident.26 By using a term associated with criminal justice, McCartney implied that a crime had been committed. By asking Blair to participate in mediation with Kanoute, she assumed that Blair was guilty of something. Within a couple of months, the independent report had exonerated Blair of any wrongdoing.

HIDDEN INJURIES

All Smith employees are now obliged to participate in anti-racism training, which requires white participants to talk about their childhood experiences of race while "confessing" to harboring racist ideas. If the capitalists studied by Marx in the nineteenth century wanted to extract as much labor as physically possible from their workers, the postindustrial boss seems to want to invade and reshape every element of their workers' psyche. How did the demand for racial justice mutate into a new form of worker discipline?

One reason may lie in the fact that PMC bosses have always been eager to find ways of sorting workers while promoting conversation about bias, rather than confronting the brutal reality of class relations and power dynamics in the workplace. Powell's New York Times report quoted one telling remark from a Smith professor: "It is safe to say race is discussed far more often than class at Smith. It's a feature of elite academic institutions that faculty and students don't recognize what it means to be elite."

PMC elites have learned that they can use the alleged racism of the white working class to justify the social stratification and economic inequality that characterize American capitalism. How else could Smith, a school allegedly focused on social justice, justify the remarkable pay differential between its president and its average employee?

In 1972, Richard Sennett and Jonathan Cobb published The Hidden Injuries of

Class, a book that summarized the findings of 150 interviews with white working-class people who lived in what the authors called "urban villages" in the Boston area, just a few hours' drive from Northampton and Smith College.28 Sennett and Cobb focused on the case of Frank Rissarro (a pseudonym), who spoke to them during their interview in a confessional mode for three hours without stopping. Rissarro was born into poverty, raised by a violent and abusive father, and had managed to attain a lower-level white-collar job at a bank: "Rissarro talked to the interviewer in a peculiar way: he treated him as an emissary from a different way of life, as a representative of a higher, more educated class, before whom he spread a justification of his entire life."

Rissarro was especially ashamed of his inability to take control of his life, to gain autonomy and satisfaction at work. He assumed that his college-educated interviewers enjoyed a dignity at work of which he was deprived. Although he displayed a casual contempt for his college-educated colleagues at the bank who had a relaxed attitude about work and no relationship to craft or manual labor, he had also internalized a sense of inferiority toward those who were more educated than him.

Sennett and Cobb treated Rissarro without judgment; he was able to speak openly to them about his life because of the empathy they displayed. However, they would prove to be exceptions to the rule for their class. College-educated elites have increasingly recoiled from lives and perspectives like Rissarro's, abjuring class as a category of analysis in favor of any other form of difference. Universities have taken to categorizing their working-class students with the more user-friendly term "first-gen," confident that a college education will differentiate their students so clearly from their families that their progeny will henceforth go on to be college-educated as well.

Fifty years after Sennett and Cobb undertook their project of interviewing working-class people in Boston's white ethnic enclaves, McCartney has proven that Rissarro was absolutely correct in assuming a defensive attitude with regard to college-educated elites. Sennett and Cobb were surprised by Rissarro's social anguish: he was a man who had escaped a violent working-class family and obtained a lower-tier white-collar job, but he could not resign himself to the emptiness and futility of his work. Unable to make peace with the culture of social mobility, Rissarro remained ambivalent about his status in the world. Sennett and

Cobb were interested in the tightly knit, insular world of the white ethnic working class in the Boston area, which revealed itself as a place where its inhabitants felt the need to prove themselves worthy of respect. The dignity afforded to the college educated was something the working class felt they constantly had to earn. This defensiveness and the injury of living in a class society that judged and shunned them forced them into tight-knit neighborhoods and communities, against which their sons and daughters eventually rebelled.

Two years after the publication of The Hidden Injuries of Class, the Boston busing riots exploded across working-class white neighborhoods forced by the state government to integrate their public schools. The ugly images of working-class whites unleashing violence against black students bused into white neighborhoods were seared into the PMC liberal imagination. White families with means moved out of Boston to the suburbs or sent their children to the many excellent private schools in the area. The white ethnic enclaves that Sennett and Cobb chose as sites for their sociological research became increasingly alienated from the world of PMC liberalism, and many working-class whites retreated into their own suburbs and the reactionary, anti–New Deal politics of Ronald Reagan.

Brown v. Board of Education was the Supreme Court case that precipitated the racial integration of the American public school system, but its insistence on equality of educational resources and student populations is a dim memory today. In our time, equality is almost never mentioned in the highly administered forms of diversity and inclusion touted by university administrators. De facto segregation, like the affinity dormitories put in place at Smith, represents a new balkanization of identity. Since the early 1970s, inequality has intensified in every American ethnic and racial category and in every stratum of American income: from African Americans to Asian Americans to income distributions across society, wealth has accrued to fewer people at the top of each group, leaving people at the center and bottom struggling to survive with compressed wages and degrading living and working conditions.

It is against a backdrop of grotesque and growing levels of economic inequality in the country that, at Smith College, the real fear experienced by Oumou Kanoute prompted the school's president to judge her staff as being existentially guilty of the sin of American racism. The gleam of the new economy and globalization may have worn off, especially after the financial collapse of 2008, but stratification continues unabated. The denigration of the working class, and of labor as a whole, allows the PMC to preside over a situation in which it serves the whims of capital but clothes itself in vainglorious colors of self-righteousness. Unable to see beyond its own self-interest, it has made social justice an individual affair that can only be adjudicated in a secular confession. In a postindustrial economy, working-class people must swallow their pride in order to adapt to serving the PMC.

At Smith, workers must be an invisible field of support for its institutional fantasy of social justice so that its students enjoy a frictionless college experience: Kanoute was not a victim of racism. She was a victim of PMC instrumentalization of race and poor, sociopathic mentoring. She learned that, by simply posting a complaint on Facebook, she could induce the college president to make an apology and have the ACLU rush to her defense. This is not a good lesson for any teenager to learn, that voicing one's suspicions can lead to the potential destruction of someone's livelihood. The investigation that exonerated the falsely accused employees will forever link Kanoute's name to a farcical drama orchestrated by a spineless college "leader," an experienced and educated woman who should have shown greater circumspection with regard to her student and her employees.

The 2018 incident at Smith allegorizes the way elites have sought to suppress discussion of working-class employment conditions in a world with a pitifully frayed social safety net. In the absence of national health care, loss of employment is nothing less than catastrophic for any worker. McCartney can disguise her abuse of power as a boss by referring to misguided and distorted ideas of campus politics and social justice, but we should ask ourselves what kind of education Smith is actually offering its students by having its president behave with impunity in this way. Furthermore, we should ask whether Smith and other institutions like it should exist at all, and what social function private colleges perform in constructing themselves as an illusory classless community, serving the principles not of education for education's sake but of cosmetic social justice, adapted to corporate America's relentless demand for allegiance and compliance to the grifter-friendly qualities of innovation and entrepreneurship.

It is time to think about dissolving private colleges and their endowments and merging them with public institutions — in Smith's case, the University of Massachusetts Amherst, a nearby public university. UMass Amherst educates 24,233 undergraduates, 77 percent of whom come from within the state. After decades of public austerity, its tuition has risen steadily, but at $15,791 for in-state students, it is less than one-third of the amount Smith charges, $55,830.31 It is already part of the Five College Consortium, including Hampshire, Smith, Mount Holyoke, and Amherst, which allows students to take courses across the five campuses.

If working toward structural equality is a liberal goal, the dissolution of private college endowments should be a step that we as a nation are willing to contemplate. Bernie Sanders proposed free public higher education for all: this is an admirable policy, but it's one that keeps the structural gap between public universities and community colleges and their elite private counterparts intact. Now is the time to be bold about imagining a different future, one founded on liberating and socializing for the public good the education and wealth that have been stockpiled and distorted by an utterly corrupt class of sycophants for capital.

Education for education's sake is the birthright of every human being. After fifty years of neoliberal education, we must strip away the veil of virtue behind which elites try to hide their deep disdain for the people over whom they rule.

Conclusion

MARX'S CAPITAL WAS A WORLD teeming with raw materials and active agents fighting and working with each other, engaged in the processes of production to wrest wealth from raw materials like gold, iron, wool, and cotton: for Marx, these workers would make history when they revolted against capitalism. PMC elite workers also see themselves as the makers of history. They labor in a world of floating signifiers, statistics, analytics, projections, predictions and identity performativity, virtue signaling, and affectual production. Their loves and lives are both virtual and disembodied. Their work continues unabated despite the ravages of the COVID-19 pandemic. People trained in this regime of symbolic manipulation love to weaponize outrage to fuel moral panics, but they are unable and unwilling to face their identity as a class. In the liberal professions, they police each other to enforce the sort of social and intellectual conformity required by their class, one that is fundamentally fragmented by competition and individualism. All PMC-approved policies about inequality, racism, and bias circle back to strengthening their sense of political agency and cultural and moral superiority. In a viciously competitive market environment, they have abandoned once cherished professional standards of research while fetishizing transgression, or better yet, the performance of transgression.

Despite its veneer of detached sophistication, the PMC embraces melodrama and sentimentality when dealing with inequality, imagining powerless people as innocent victims who it alone is uniquely able to "help." The PMC desperately wants to be a gender-neutral Atticus Finch. For Marx, the unique industrial processes of labor formed the vanguard class of industrial capitalism. Managers and professionals were unfortunately never part of that class, but their complicity with capital is something they want to disguise as "resilience" and "flexibility," qualities that working-class losers do not possess in the PMC worldview. Workers remade the industrial world, but today's PMC elites resent the revolutionary power of the leftism of the past. They want to manage social change and a possible revolution even as their own functions are constrained by the ideological demands of the ruling class. Even though they understand the futility of their own work, they do not believe in the systemic changes necessary to remake economic systems that would allow the many to find rewarding work and lead meaningful lives of dignity and economic security.

In historicizing the PMC's ideological investments, I am not simply trying to "understand" its identity to add to a precious repository of scholastic knowledge. I am interested in criticizing its values in order to abandon its politics. To build a socialist future, we have to engage in a constant struggle to overcome the political paralysis to which both centrism and pseudo-radicalism lead. Across the world, ordinary people without college degrees have rejected PMC technocracy in favor of populist authoritarianism because they no longer believe in the dominant neoliberal narrative about austerity and competition. To the majority of non-college-educated people, the PMC increasingly appear as pedantic, hypocritical, and punishing: in authoritarian, science denying conservative leaders, they recognize their own helpless rage and ignorance. In angry demagogues, they find the embodiment of a sovereignty they have been denied. Of course, their support for billionaire populists and their minions is entirely reactionary, but the political answer to populism is not liberal reformism or moderate centrism. It is committed socialism. If the PMC still insists that a little bit of economic redistribution should be managed carefully by corporate friendly "experts," socialists have to demand a different order of politics and a different calculation of political engagement, one which aims at building solidarity in the shadow of a distant revolutionary horizon.

Dear reader, you are probably like me, a member of the PMC, or at least you have been educated in its institutions. I hope that this short introduction to the false consciousness of a class that still wants to believe itself a heroic and virtuous political actor will strengthen the reader's resolve to reject PMC politics while building on this critique of its reactionary class positions. Having been imbued with its ethos and its ideology, we all have to work to undo the effects of PMC propaganda to join the class war from below. This brief introduction serves as a guide to identifying PMC values in ourselves, the better to liquidate them. Because of the ideological distortions of leftist politics by PMC values, self-criticism must be the beginning of all political engagement. We have to abandon the way the PMC wants us to think about success, intelligence, racism, violence, children, reading, health care, well-being, pleasure, and sex. We have to reject making a virtue out of taste and consumption habits. We have to understand ourselves as the universal subject of a history dominated by capitalism's dynamic, exploitative, and punishing powers. It will not be easy, because PMC elites control so much of our lives and quietly threaten us with exclusion if we do not follow their sanctioned lines of milquetoast politics.

The PMC would have us forget that as a class, it has served capitalism and the profit motive very well: tragically, it has also been hugely successful at monopolizing the language of progressive and enlightened politics, even as it has abandoned the best aspects of liberal professionalism and the democratic culture in which such ideas of intellectual autonomy can thrive. The values of professionalism, with its disinterested call for accountability and respect of truths arrived at by a community of researchers, are critical to building socialism. Professionalism is not the enemy of solidarity. Professionalism and its disciplinary limits are necessary for nurturing socialist specialists who will be needed to oversee massive economic redistribution and the strengthening of public infrastructure and public goods that will be necessary for the environmental survival of the planet and the political survival of democracy.

I am finishing this manuscript in the middle of the coronavirus pandemic lockdown. The economic and public health disaster that we are experiencing in the United States is directly linked to the power of for-profit health care interests and corporations in hollowing out public services and public health. The fact that the Biden–Harris administration is opposed to national health care, or Medicare for All, is very revealing. Rather than promoting national health care, a phalanx of centrist experts will promote individual actions, such as mask wearing, as the new "virtues." Yes, we should wear masks, but we should demand free COVID-19 testing and contact tracing, free vaccines along with the rebuilding of public health institutions to serve public health and not the profit motive. If times go back to normal, and your boss or health insurer tries to sell you on the commodification of your health as a "wellness" protocol, remember that health care is part of public infrastructure, not a commodity. Just as provision for quality childcare for every family should be part of public infrastructure, so should the care of the elderly and the sick be priority areas of public investment. My goal is simple: help normalize socialist economics and politics in the face of the concerted demonization of its vision of what is collectively possible. Socialism itself is neither glamorous nor innovative: it does not sprinkle its agendas with new pronouns or fancy neologisms. Its signifiers do not float on air or ether: its policies should be tethered to good statistics, objective reality, and the power and uncertainty of scientific method and reason. A socialist intellectual should refuse to wear the cloaks of virtue, erudition, and detachment: she should be prepared to enter the field of class struggle on the side of workers and the exploited. Conservative and progressive PMC elites and the institutions they control are actively hostile to worker power and socialism as such. Therefore solidarity and organization are more critical than ever to long-term political struggle. Affect-driven protests, raucous crowds, and violent rioting may provide the political openings for social change, but political transformation at the scale we need demands discipline of the kind the academic Left is used to condemning. While a mixed economy may be the short-term reality that we dare hope for, let's strengthen the hand of the socialist aspects of that hybrid system. While the PMC promotes the hoarding of capital and virtue, we must detach ourselves from its crypto-Puritanical regulation of human appetites and human relations. We must be heretics. We should blaspheme.

The PMC elite has refused to name the economic system that has ruined our planet, undermined our trust in public institutions, destroyed public health, diminished our childhoods, and litigated our pleasures. Neither evil nor virtuous, the PMC is a secular and material antagonist. In calling out capitalism as the enemy of the people, we must also name our enemy's most assiduous courtier and sycophant: the professional managerial class.

译者后记

这本《美德占有者》是南加州大学欧文分校凯瑟琳娜·刘教授的一本站在工人阶级立场批判美国专业管理阶级、富有马克思主义和社会主义精神的美国社会观察著作。其从社会学、经济学、历史学的视角、马克思主义哲学的批判角度，对美国社会结构中的深层次矛盾进行了剖析，指出专业管理阶级背叛了人民中的大多数，站在1%的富人一边帮助剥削工人阶级，脱离群众而占领道德制高点，同时，因为他们自己所塑造的阶级壁垒，他们自身也生活在阶级滑落的焦虑之中。

凯瑟琳娜·刘教授的《美德占有者》反映了美国精英群体怎样的困境？

美国的自由主义者试图用美德的冲突来掩盖阶级冲突，例如，他们认为穷人相比富人更缺乏自控力。事实上，美德只是用来规训PMC（专业管理阶级）以及穷人的工具，掌握权力和资本之后，人的自控力等美德反而会急转直下。这一套逻辑在世界范围内仍然适用，而PMC的矛盾在于，他们的工作是帮助既得利益者维护"教育、法律、医疗"领域的规则，以获得社会结构的稳定和持续的收益，但他们自己也是被剥削的对象，仍然是1%VS 99%里面的后者。无论是阶级滑落，还是他们对于孩子教育的焦虑，都在证明一点，那就是所谓的专业管理阶级充其量是羊群里的领头羊，对于牧羊人来说，领头羊只要够用就好，不服从或者表现不佳的领头羊同样会成为餐桌上的涮羊肉。

凯瑟琳娜对于身份政治的批评，或者说对于自由主义将人类按照"文化团体"属性进行分类的不满，归根到底是对"人类该如何被分类"问题另一回答的强调——马克思主义，这种按照阶级分类的思考，其最大的优势在于"务实"，以资本和权力为根本关切。

道德不仅仅是尼采所说的"弱者的武器"，同样也是用于控制弱者的"强者的武器"。当一件事，强者和弱者都需要时，它才能够跨越时间的河流，经久不衰。

自2019年我与凯瑟琳娜·刘教授在洛杉矶相识，已经过去4年，我们一直保持着对于马克思主义和社会主义在当今美国社会堪忧状况的讨论与关注。她是一位战士，用她自己的话说就是"她在专业管理阶级掌控的大学接受了教育，但仍然坚信只有社会主义才能解决美国的社会问题"。秉持着这样的信念，最终我们决定将她的这本著作和她的一些本土的思考以译著的方式向马克思主义热土——中国的读者展示出来，以期获得更多的交流、碰撞和支持。

我要对郑恩和千叶万希子两位译者表示衷心的感谢，他们的专业知识和努力为本书的完成贡献了巨大力量；同时，也感谢协助我的几位学生——操勇军、周奕鋆、谭颖、何曼婷、康佳怡，他们的认真、踏实、好学令我印象深刻，我很开心能与他们在此次翻译工作中共同成长。此外，我还要感谢中国传媒大学出版社的裴向敏编辑及其他工作人员的辛勤付出，是你们的耐心与不懈努力才使此译著能够顺利面向中国读者。

张　焱
2023年10月于乡村振兴途中

图书在版编目（CIP）数据

美德占有者：对抗专业管理阶级的案例 /（美）凯瑟琳娜·刘著；张焱，郑恩，（日）千叶万希子译. -- 北京：中国传媒大学出版社，2023.9

书名原文：Virtue Hoarders: the case against the professional managerial class

ISBN 978-7-5657-3436-6

Ⅰ.①美… Ⅱ.①凯… ②张… ③郑… ④千… Ⅲ.①管理社会学 Ⅳ.① C936

中国国家版本馆 CIP 数据核字（2023）第 115542 号

Licensed by the University of Minnesota Press, Minneapolis, Minnesota, U.S.A

Copyright © 2021 by Catherine Liu

美德占有者——对抗专业管理阶级的案例

MEIDE ZHANYOUZHE—DUIKANG ZHUANYE GUANLI JIEJI DE ANLI

著　　者	[美] 凯瑟琳娜·刘	
译　　者	张焱　郑恩　[日] 千叶万希子	
策划编辑	裴向敏	
责任编辑	裴向敏	
封面设计	拓美设计	
责任印制	李志鹏	
出版发行	中国传媒大学出版社	
社　　址	北京市朝阳区定福庄东街 1 号	邮　编　100024
电　　话	86-10-65450528　65450532	传　真　65779405
网　　址	http://cucp.cuc.edu.cn	
经　　销	全国新华书店	
印　　刷	唐山玺诚印务有限公司	
开　　本	710mm×1000mm　　1/16	
印　　张	11	
字　　数	145 千字	
版　　次	2023 年 9 月第 1 版	
印　　次	2023 年 9 月第 1 次印刷	
书　　号	ISBN 978-7-5657-3436-6/C·3436	定　价　55.00 元

本社法律顾问：北京嘉润律师事务所　郭建平